THE EDITORS OF *TEXAS MONTHLY* CELEBRATE THE EVER-EVOLVING CULINARY LANDSCAPE OF THE LONE STAR STATE IN THIS STUNNING COOKBOOK, FEATURING MORE THAN ONE HUNDRED RECIPES.

When it comes to food, Texas may be best known for its beloved barbecue and tacos. But with more than twenty-nine million residents, the state is one of the most culturally diverse in America—and so is its culinary scene. From the kolaches introduced by Czech settlers to the Hill Country in the 1800s to the Viet-Cajun crawfish Vietnamese immigrants blessed Houston with in the early 2000s, the tastes on offer are as vast and varied as the 268,596 square miles of earth they spring from.

In *The Big Texas Cookbook*, the editors of the award-winning magazine *Texas Monthly* have gathered an expansive collection of recipes that reflects the state's food traditions, eclectically grouped by how Texans like to start and end the day (Rise and Shine, There Stands the Glass); how they revere their native-born ingredients (Made in Texas); and how they love the people, places, and rituals that surround their cherished meals (On Holiday, Home Plates). Getting their very own chapters—no surprise—are the behemoths mentioned above, barbecue and Tex-Mex (Smoke Signals, Con Todo). With recipes for über-regional specialties like venison parisa, home-cooking favorites like King Ranch casserole, and contemporary riffs like a remarkable Lao Texas chili, *The Big Texas Cookbook* pays homage to the cooks who long ago shaped the state's culinary culture and the ones who are building on those traditions in surprising and delightful ways.

The
Big Texas
Cookbook

ALSO BY THE EDITORS
OF *TEXAS MONTHLY*

Being Texan

The Big Texas Cookbook

The Editors of

TexasMonthly

HARPER WAVE

An Imprint of HarperCollins*Publishers*

"Food is about many things—nourishment, pleasure, and culture among them—but it's also about recognizing who you are, and why."
—*Patricia Sharpe*

The Big Texas Cookbook is dedicated to all Texans who recognize themselves within it.

Contents

BY DAN GOODGAME

Introduction

Any mention of Texas cooking seems to conjure, in the popular imagination, dishes that could have been served off the back of a chuck wagon in a Hollywood western: sizzling steaks, juicy smoked brisket, spicy chili, and perhaps an early version of fajitas. Those are beloved staples here, to be sure. But our cuisine has always been more eclectic and braided.

Consider that in 1883, when the population of Houston was about twenty thousand, when only one building boasted electric lighting and most of the city's streets were mud, the Ladies' Association of the First Presbyterian Church assembled a collection of its members' "receipts," as recipes then were called. They amassed directions for making 721 dishes, from parsnip fritters and pig's-head hash to chili sauce and baked cashaw (a succulent squash from Mexico). As a bonus, they threw in eighty homemaking tips and remedies, including a potent cough syrup containing honey, licorice, and opium.

They priced the book at $1.50—around $40 today. The preface noted that cookbooks published elsewhere "contain receipts not suited to the requirements of our climate" and added that "as far as we know, no complete treatise on the subject of cookery has been published in our latitude." Thus was born what is generally acknowledged to be the first Texas cookbook. It would not be the last. In a closet at the *Texas Monthly* offices, Pat Sharpe, our veteran dining critic, has access to a dozen shelves full of the things, which I find appropriate for a state so vast and rapidly evolving.

Like the rest of our culture, Texas cuisine has been shaped by the waves of immigration that have washed over this territory since the first

Indigenous bands roamed and settled it. Each cohort of new arrivals blessed us with a wealth of ingredients and dishes, including from all parts of Mexico. In the 1800s, German immigrants brought, among other delicacies, hearty breads and sausages, along with cuttings to grow wine grapes. Czechs introduced kolaches and klobasniky. Blacks and whites from the Deep South contributed everything from fried chicken to collard greens and field peas. Cajuns added gumbos and étouffées.

More recent waves of newcomers have helped longtime Texans develop an appreciation for the foods of India, Iran, Lebanon, Nigeria, and Vietnam. And in the past few years, we've seen delightful mash-ups such as barbecued-pork banh mi, gumbo tacos, Lao Texas chili, and grilled Moroccan carrots. That last item is offered by some of our top barbecue joints, and it's part of a trend incisively reported by Daniel Vaughn, our barbecue editor. Upstart pitmasters, many of whom apprenticed under legends such as Aaron Franklin, are smoking and grilling everything from lamb and octopus to cauliflower. Yet they also venerate and serve the Texas Trinity of brisket, pork ribs, and sausage.

That ethos—of respect for Texas traditions alongside exuberant sampling of everything new—is what inspired this cookbook. We believe, with characteristic Lone Star exceptionalism, that *Texas Monthly* is uniquely qualified to pull it off. We've been chronicling the state, including its restaurants and home cooking, for fifty years. We're the only magazine in the known universe to employ both a full-time barbecue editor and taco editor, not to mention a fine-dining critic who's seen a few rodeos during her four-plus decades on

the job. Each is regarded as a national authority. Our contributors include experts on the state's burgeoning selection of homegrown beers, wines, spirits, and cocktails. Heck, even our political reporters end up writing about the new foods they discover during their travels.

For this book, we've selected reader favorites from among the hundreds of classic Texas recipes we've published over the past half century, for dishes such as chicken-fried steak, King Ranch casserole, nachos, and queso. And since launching this project, we've traveled the state afresh to collect, from home cooks and chefs alike, a sampling of the most exciting new offerings that reflects Texas's growing culinary diversity. Anyone for a steaming bowl of joumou, a Haitian oxtail stew, as interpreted by Houston chef Jonny Rhodes? And maybe some chawanmushi custard?

Texas Monthly is all about storytelling, so among this book's one hundred recipes, we've woven excerpts from classic articles, along with new essays. Some writers tell of favorite foods from their Texan childhoods; others of discovering the state's cuisine as adults. Dan Solomon shares

why he enjoys celebrating Thanksgiving at Luby's Cafeteria, a treasured institution in our state. Alongside a formula for pickling peppers, Alison Cook notes: "If Texans hold any truth to be self-evident, it is that there is nothing that would not be improved by the addition of a little jalapeño." Emily McCullar, an eleventh-generation Texan, observes that "the pecan became our official state tree in 1919, and it produces the only nut Texans grow commercially (if you don't count our politicians, that is)."

My favorite cookbooks, including Madhur Jaffrey's *From Curries to Kebabs* and Hank Shaw's *Buck, Buck, Moose*, are ones I prize both for delicious and carefully tested recipes and for the pleasure of the stories they contain. Through Jaffrey's book, I learned more not only about India's cooking but also about its many regions and cultures. I hope this book, in similar fashion, provides an array of exciting new dishes to try as well as a deeper appreciation of what Texas has been and is becoming.

CHAPTER 1

Made
in
Texas

BY EMILY McCULLAR

From Field to Stream and Beyond

Even as a small child, I knew enough to hope that my father and his friends would each "bag the limit" (fifteen birds) in their annual dove hunt. They would pool their spoils and throw a celebratory dinner, and the more fowl they killed, the more room they had for us freeloaders (aka their wives and kids). Those little birds were always prepared the same delectable way: stuffed with cream cheese and jalapeño, then wrapped in bacon and grilled. We all wanted a seat at that table.

Dove poppers were just one of the gamy delicacies that defined my Central Texas upbringing. We ate deer sausage, green-chile feral hog, and fried wild turkey tenders. There was always something extra holy about foods acquired out in the field, which could materialize only if a hunter displayed some skill and found a lotta luck. I realized this experience was not universal when I went to college on the East Coast, where I encountered city kids who'd never eaten venison nor wanted to. My outsized Texas pride was already fully formed; there it would expand to include our treasured culinary traditions.

Of course, wild game is not the only staple of our collective palate. This cookbook is proof that our tastes are many and motley. But there are certain foodstuffs that stand out as deeply Texan. They are our homegrown heroes, literally—the flora and fauna that have made this part of the world a site of human settlement for centuries. They include not only white-tailed deer and white-winged dove but also Fredericksburg peaches, San Saba pecans, and all the redfish and oysters the Gulf of Mexico can provide. Throughout the decades, hungry Texans have taken these ingredients and turned them into classic dishes, meals as entwined with Texas identity as the cowboy boot.

Consider the pecan. It's native to North America, but many experts believe the tree originated here,

in Texas, some sixty-five million years ago. Pecans featured prominently in the cuisine of Indigenous cultures and helped Cabeza de Vaca survive the winter when he was shipwrecked on the coast in 1532. The pecan became our official state tree in 1919, and it produces the only nut Texans grow commercially (if you don't count our politicians, that is). I bet there are pecan pralines for sale at every cash register in every gas station in this whole state. I've never been to a holiday gathering that didn't have at least one pecan pie; usually, there are several. We put pecans everywhere. We sprinkle them atop sheet cakes and crush them into cookies the color of Permian sand because they're Texan, and they're ours.

Which brings me to chili, our beloved "bowl of red," a dish that inspires much passion (particularly when it comes to the misguided inclusion of beans). It too is a product of Texas's storied past. As the lore tells it, the chili we know was born in nineteenth-century San Antonio, where enterprising Tejanas sold stews of red meat and spicy peppers on the city's plazas. It later spread throughout the rest of the state via the cattle drives, where there was always plenty of beef and a chuck wagon full of dried chiles.

These days, every proud Texan has a preferred recipe, or at least a strong opinion about one. My Lovelady-born grandfather, who spent much of his adulthood in the Midwest, went as far as to teach a St. Louis butcher how to properly cube the chuck. That grandfather has been dead for more than twenty years, but my family still shares that anecdote. A Texan's love of chili isn't just about the flavor or how it delights the senses. When a food comes to embody a history—be it societal or familial—the very idea of it is cherished.

And because we're Texans, because we take ownership of almost everything that comes from here, because we tie our identities to these things in a way that genuinely annoys people from outta state (bless their hearts), these aren't just foods we like. These foods are ours.

Texas Quail with Fig Mole

Houston's Hugo Ortega is the winner of the 2017 James Beard Best Chef Southwest award, as well as the patriarch of a family empire of Mexican restaurants that includes Xochi, Hugo's, and Caracol. In this recipe, he employs earthy wild mushrooms and a fruit-forward mole for a fresh take on Texas's beloved game bird.

Serves 6

For the mushroom stuffing
(makes about 3 cups)

2 tablespoons vegetable oil

3 tablespoons finely diced white onion

1 garlic clove, minced

1½ pounds assorted mushrooms, such as button, shiitake, wood ear, and chanterelle, woody parts of the stems trimmed, chopped

Salt

½ teaspoon ground black pepper

2 tablespoons chopped fresh flat-leaf parsley

For the fig mole (makes 2 quarts)

6 ancho chiles, stems and seeds removed

3 pasilla chiles, stems and seeds removed

3 mulato chiles, stems and seeds removed

6 green tomatillos, husks removed

1 medium white onion, roughly chopped

4 garlic cloves, peeled

¼ cup vegetable oil

2 cups fresh figs, stems removed

1 cup dried Black Mission figs

1 cup dried apricots

1 teaspoon whole cumin seeds

5 whole allspice berries

5 whole cloves

2 dried avocado leaves (see Note)

1 teaspoon dried oregano

½ cup sesame seeds

½ stick Mexican cinnamon

TO MAKE THE STUFFING:

Heat the oil in a large, heavy skillet over medium heat. Add the onion and cook, stirring constantly, for 20 seconds, then add the garlic and cook for 10 more seconds. Add the mushrooms and cook, continuing to stir, until the mushrooms are wilted and begin to caramelize. Season with the salt and pepper and sprinkle with the parsley. Transfer to a bowl and set aside to cool.

TO MAKE THE MOLE:

Heat a large cast-iron skillet over medium heat. Add the chiles in a single layer and toast for 2 to 3 minutes, turning constantly, until the color darkens. Take care not to burn them. Remove from the pan and set aside.

Add the tomatillos to the same pan and roast until the skin starts to show black blisters; turn over and do the same with the other side. Remove from the pan and set aside.

Use the same pan to roast the onion and garlic, moving them around constantly until they start to get black spots. Set aside.

Heat a heavy-bottomed pot or Dutch oven over medium heat. Add the oil, fresh and dried figs, and apricots and cook for 2 minutes, stirring constantly. Add the cumin seeds, allspice, cloves, avocado leaves, oregano, sesame seeds, cinnamon, roasted tomatillos, chiles, onion, and garlic and cook for 2 minutes.

Add the vegetable stock, cover, and bring to a simmer. Reduce the heat to low and cook for 25 minutes. Remove the avocado leaves and cinnamon stick. Blend the mixture in a blender to

(cont.)

2 quarts vegetable stock

1 tablespoon sugar

Salt

For the quail

6 semi-boneless quail

Salt and ground black pepper

3 cups wild mushroom stuffing (see above)

6 slices thinly cut bacon

2 tablespoons vegetable oil

Fig mole (see above), warmed
(about ½ cup per quail on the plate,
with additional sauce in a bowl
on the table)

a smooth consistency in a few batches, covering the top with a towel.

Pour the mole into a wide pot and cook over low heat for 30 minutes, stirring frequently to avoid sticking to the bottom of the pot. Add the sugar. Taste and add salt as needed.

TO MAKE THE QUAIL:

While the mole is cooking, preheat the oven to 350°F.

Season the quail all over with salt and pepper. Divide the mushroom stuffing into 6 equal parts (about ½ cup each) and use it to stuff the quail. Wrap each quail (around the breast) with one piece of bacon and secure the ends of the bacon with a toothpick.

Heat the vegetable oil in a large cast-iron skillet over medium heat. When hot, place the quail breast-side down and cook for 3 minutes on each side. Once all the quail are cooked, place in a baking dish and roast for 10 minutes.

Remove from the oven and allow to rest for 5 minutes. Serve with a ladleful of the warmed fig mole on the plate, with additional sauce in a bowl on the side.

Note: Dried avocado leaves are available in the spice aisle of grocery stores that specialize in Mexican cooking. They're also available online.

Venison Parisa

Similar in preparation to a steak tartare, parisa is an über-regional (Medina County, in the Hill Country) dish of raw meat mixed with onion and cheese and served with crackers. Beef is traditional, but Janie Ramirez, the executive chef of Dai Due, in Austin, prefers the silky texture of hand-chopped venison loin for her parisa, which she calls "deer camp power food." She also incorporates jalapeños, of course. She recommends freezing the meat to facilitate chopping, then letting the dish marinate for an hour or two. And she warns that it should be served with either Ritz or saltine crackers but not both: "There are two distinct and contentious camps in the appropriate parisa cracker world, so you must pick a side. I am on Team Ritz."

Serves 4

1 pound venison loin, tenderloin, or heart, well cleaned and trimmed of all fat and silverskin

¼ cup pickled or fresh jalapeño chiles, finely chopped

Salt and ground black pepper

Zest and juice of 2 to 3 medium limes

1 tablespoon olive oil

1 cup grated cheddar cheese

Ritz or saltine crackers, for serving

Freeze the meat for 20 minutes, then cut it with a sharp knife into ¼-inch slices. Cut these into strips, then dice. Finely chop the diced meat, using the blade to turn the meat over and over until it reaches almost a ground consistency. Add the chiles, season with salt and pepper, and give it a couple more passes with the knife.

Transfer the seasoned meat to a bowl and add most of the lime zest and juice, the oil, and the cheese. Check the seasoning and add the remaining lime zest and juice and more salt if needed.

Wrap the parisa tightly in plastic wrap and refrigerate for at least 1 hour before serving with the crackers of your choice.

Note: This recipe also works well with elk, moose, nilgai, and antelope.

Jalapeño Dove Poppers

Say the words *jalapeño dove poppers* to a hunter and you'll see a smile spread from ear to ear. But just looking at a plateful—with crisp bacon wrapped around each meaty, pepper-spiked dove breast, cream cheese oozing decadently around the edges—will bring tears of joy to any Texan's eyes.

Makes 30 poppers

15 whole, plucked dove breasts

1 teaspoon garlic salt

1 teaspoon ground black pepper

2 (12-ounce) packages bacon
(not thick-cut)

1 (8-ounce) package cream cheese

15 jalapeño chile slices
(fresh or canned), each slice
cut into half-moons

Prepare a grill to medium-high heat. If you're cooking over wood, use mesquite or oak. If using a charcoal grill, allow the flames to die down and cook over hot coals.

Use a paring knife to separate the dove breasts from the breast bones to make thirty lobes. Sprinkle with the garlic salt and black pepper.

Cut each slice of bacon in half. Take a breast lobe, top with a spoonful of cream cheese and a half-moon slice of chile, and wrap in bacon. Secure the bacon ends with a toothpick.

Grill for 3 to 5 minutes, then turn. Continue grilling until the bacon is crisp, an additional 3 to 5 minutes.

Crawfish Boil, Two Ways

Every spring, little mudbugs become a big deal in Southeast Texas, where they are consumed Cajun-style, in which the freshwater crustaceans get their seasoning from the boil itself, and Viet-Cajun style, in which the critters go from the boil pot to a flavor bath of spicy garlic butter. Invite your pals to belly up to a newspaper-lined table in the backyard, because it's time to get peeling.

This recipe is meant to be repeated per 10 pounds of crawfish. Over an outdoor propane burner, we boiled a 30-pound sack in a 30-quart pot in 3 batches, which served 6 to 10 people. Measurements are loose; customize to your taste.

10 pounds live crawfish

4 to 5 cups seafood boil mix, such as Zatarain's

5 heads garlic, halved horizontally

1 pound (4 sticks) unsalted butter

5 pounds red potatoes (optional)

6 ears corn, shucked and cut crosswise into 3-inch chunks (optional)

1 orange, cut into slices, peel and all

Rinse the crawfish with fresh water (in a cooler or maybe a kiddie pool) two or three times, until the water runs clear.

Fill the largest pot you own with water, about one-third to halfway up the side (you want just enough to cover the bugs) and turn the heat on to high. As the water heats up, add 2 cups of the seafood boil mix, the garlic, and ½ pound (2 sticks) of the butter. Bring to a boil.

If you're cooking potatoes and corn too, add the potatoes first, then add the corn about 15 minutes later. Once the corn is in, cover the pot and cook for 10 minutes. Remove the veggies from the pot, sprinkle with a little boil mix if you like, and keep them warm.

Next add 2 or 3 more cups of boil mix (depending on how spicy you like your crawfish), the orange slices, and the remaining ½ pound (2 sticks) butter. Return to a boil, then dump in 10 pounds of crawfish. Give them a hearty stir, cover the pot, and cook for 5 to 7 minutes.

When the crawfish are done (they will turn bright red and start to float), use a wire-mesh skimmer to scoop them out and dump them into a big cooler. Repeat for any additional batches. Once all the crawfish are cooked, serve in a large pile directly on a newspaper-lined table outdoors. Provide plenty of containers for disposing of shells, as well as lots of napkins.

Viet-Cajun Style

Viet-Cajun crawfish is distinguished by a post-boil toss in spicy garlic butter and lively dipping sauces, some of which are said to have been born of unfettered access to restaurant condiment stations.

1 pound (4 sticks) unsalted butter

1 head garlic, peeled and chopped (about 20 cloves)

2 tablespoons Cajun seasoning

Juice of 2 lemons

In a medium saucepan, combine the butter, garlic, and Cajun seasoning and set the heat to medium. Once the butter melts, reduce the heat to low and simmer for 3 to 4 minutes. Add the lemon juice and remove from the heat.

Working in batches, toss the cooked crawfish with garlic butter in a large bowl or plastic bag. Serve as is or with these popular dipping sauces.

- A sriracha-style sauce that combines equal parts ketchup and mayonnaise with cayenne pepper to taste

- Lemon juice mixed with cayenne pepper to taste

- Muối tiêu chanh: 2 parts salt and 1 part white pepper mixed with fresh lime juice to taste

Note: For a Laotian spin, serve with the jeow som on page 144.

Fried Catfish

The homely catfish has always had an image problem, what with his fleshy lips, squooshy skin, and propensity for eating off the river bottom. But none of that has ever bothered Texans; we eat a heck of a lot of it, and casting about for channels and blues and frying them up in a cast-iron pot is a veritable rite of passage for many of us.

Serves 4

2 cups whole milk

1 teaspoon hot sauce

2 cups finely ground cornmeal

4 teaspoons kosher salt

2 teaspoons ground black pepper

2 teaspoons paprika

1 teaspoon cayenne pepper

2 pounds catfish fillets (about 4; can be cut into smaller fillets or tenders)

Peanut oil, for frying

Lemon wedges, for serving

In a shallow bowl, stir together the milk and hot sauce. In another shallow bowl, combine the cornmeal, salt, pepper, paprika, and cayenne.

Dip the fish in the milk, then dredge in the cornmeal mixture, coating thoroughly.

Let sit for a few minutes while you heat about 2 inches of oil to 350°F in a deep cast-iron pot (a thermometer is immensely helpful in maintaining the oil temperature; adjust the heat accordingly).

When the oil is hot, gently add the fish (a few pieces at a time—don't crowd the pot) and fry, flipping halfway through, until golden brown on both sides, 3 to 4 minutes. Let drain on paper towels and serve with lemon wedges.

Grilled Oysters

The Gulf of Mexico is home to the largest remaining wild oyster reefs in the world, and Texans have long appreciated the meaty mollusks: raw and fried, in gumbos, and, of course, on the grill, where their flame-kissed shells serve as vessels in which they poach themselves in their own liquor (and maybe a little chile butter).

Makes 2 dozen

For the compound butter

½ cup (1 stick) unsalted butter, softened

1 garlic clove, minced

1 jalapeño chile, stem and seeds removed, diced

1 tablespoon chopped fresh cilantro

Juice of 1 lime (about 2 tablespoons)

Salt and ground black pepper

For the oysters

2 dozen Gulf oysters in their shells

Hot sauce and saltines, for serving

TO MAKE THE COMPOUND BUTTER:

Place all the ingredients in a bowl and stir until incorporated.

TO MAKE THE OYSTERS:

Get a hot fire going on the grill (charcoal is best if you want that smoky flavor).

Give your oysters a good scrubbing, discarding any with broken or open shells. Shuck, removing and discarding the top shell and placing the oyster along with its liquor in the deeper shell.

Get all your shucks in a row on a large sheet pan, add a little nubbin of your compound butter to each one, and head for the grill. Gently place the oysters on the grill (in batches, if you have a bunch), close the lid, and leave for about 3 minutes. Then take a peek; you'll want to see the edges of the oysters starting to curl up a little and the butter getting brown and bubbly. Don't overcook; they shouldn't take more than 4 or 5 minutes.

Carefully remove from the grill—don't spill the juice!—and arrange on a bed of rock salt (if you want to be fancy). Serve with hot sauce, saltines, and beer.

Seafood Gumbo

Think gumbo and you think Louisiana, and rightfully so. But anyone who lives along the Gulf Coast knows that borders down there are as murky as this mucilaginous mother of all stews. *Texas Monthly*'s editor in chief, Dan Goodgame, shares this recipe from his mother, Betty, and his step-grandmother, Gertrude Delmas, a descendant of one of the French families that founded Dan's hometown of Pascagoula, Mississippi. "Before landing in Pascagoula," he says, "the Delmas clan had traveled through Haiti and Louisiana, and they learned a great deal about Creole cooking in all three places. Main streets in both Port au Prince and Pascagoula bear the Delmas name—as do many pages of the police arrest blotter at the Cabildo in New Orleans."

Serves 8 to 10

2 pounds head-on shrimp

Salt

3 quarts (12 cups) shrimp or chicken stock

2 tablespoons olive oil

1 pound fresh okra (see Note), cut crosswise into ½-inch coins

½ pound andouille or other smoked sausage, cut into ½-inch coins

½ cup (1 stick) unsalted butter

6 tablespoons all-purpose flour

1 large yellow onion, diced (about 3 cups)

1 green bell pepper, stem and seeds removed, diced (about 1½ cups)

5 celery stalks, diced (about 1½ cups)

6 garlic cloves, roughly chopped (about 2 tablespoons)

2½ cups diced fresh tomatoes (or one 28-ounce can diced tomatoes)

1 tablespoon ground thyme

1 teaspoon ground black pepper

1 teaspoon cayenne pepper

1 pint fresh jumbo lump crabmeat

1 pint fresh oysters, drained

Hot cooked white rice, for serving

1 bunch green onions, finely chopped (about 1 cup)

1 cup finely chopped fresh flat-leaf parsley

Filé (optional), for serving

Remove and reserve the tails, shells, and heads from your shrimp. Refrigerate the shrimp, then add the tails, shells, and heads to a large pot along with a big pinch of salt and the stock. Bring the stock to a simmer and let simmer as you prepare the other ingredients. (Do not let it come to a boil; if it does, it will turn bitter.)

Heat a large, heavy-bottomed pot or Dutch oven over medium-high heat; add 1 tablespoon of the oil, the okra, and a healthy pinch of salt. (To avoid crowding the pot, you may need to cook the okra in two batches.) Cook, stirring frequently, until the okra begins to brown and there are no longer strings of slime when you stir it, about 5 minutes. Use a slotted spoon to remove and set aside.

In the same pot, brown the sliced andouille on both sides, about 2 minutes per side. Remove from the pot.

Turn the heat down to medium-low and add the butter and the remaining 1 tablespoon oil to the pot. When the butter has melted, whisk in the flour to make a smooth, thin paste. Switch to a wooden spoon, add a big pinch of salt, and cook, stirring constantly, until the roux is a caramel brown color, about 40 minutes.

Add the onion, then the bell pepper and celery, and then the garlic to the pot, stirring between each addition. Cook the vegetables, stirring frequently, until softened but not browned, about 8 minutes.

(cont.)

Strain the stock through a mesh strainer. Gradually ladle in just enough stock so that the bottom of the pot is covered; stir until the lumps in the roux smooth out. Repeat—adding about the same amount of liquid each time, then stirring until smooth and letting the mixture heat back up—until you've incorporated all the stock. It should be, as Dan's mama says, "too thick to drink and too thin to plow." The gumbo will thicken further as it cooks.

Add the tomatoes, the sautéed okra, and the browned sausage. Add the ground thyme, black pepper, cayenne, and 1 teaspoon salt. Stir to combine and bring to a simmer.

Cook at a low simmer, stirring frequently, for about 1 hour. (It's fine to let it simmer up to several hours at this point, if you like.)

Add the shrimp and cook until the shrimp are curled and pink, about 3 minutes. Add the crabmeat and oysters and adjust the seasonings to your taste. Bring back to a simmer and cook until the oyster edges ruffle, about 2 minutes.

Serve immediately over white rice, garnished with green onions, parsley, and filé, if desired. Remove any leftovers from the heat and cover until everybody is ready for seconds.

Note: Frozen or canned okra works as well; drain canned okra before using.

Redfish on the Half Shell

Sport fishermen have long intoned the joys of stalking this tenacious resident of the Gulf of Mexico. Fittingly, Texas's official saltwater fish continues to put up a fight even after it's dispatched, in the form of scales so hard to remove that most cooks don't even bother. They just cut it in half lengthwise, gut it, and grill it as is, letting the skin and scales serve as a smoky "shell" from which to spoon mild, meaty flesh that graciously submits to all kinds of seasonings.

Serves 2

2 redfish fillets, with skin and scales
(a fishmonger will prepare this properly
if you tell them what you're making)

2 tablespoons Cajun seasoning (see Note)

1 lemon

Check the fish for pin bones by lightly running your hand over the exposed surface of the fish. Remove any bones you feel poking through (a pair of tweezers helps).

Season the exposed side of the fillets with the Cajun seasoning.

Over a hot grill, cook the fish skin-side down for 10 to 20 minutes, depending on thickness, until it is opaque and flakes easily with a fork.

Juice the lemon over the fillets and use a large spoon to scoop the fish from the skin.

Note: Most Cajun seasoning blends contain salt already. If yours does not, sprinkle the fillets with the seasoning and a large pinch of salt.

Competition-Style Texas Chili

The legendary chili cookoffs of Texas are known for strict rules (no beans!) and fierce competition. To win, cooks eliminate as many variables as possible in their recipes, meaning you'll see lots of dried and canned ingredients, which preclude the risk of encountering an inferior tomato or onion on cookoff day. Spices are added in separate "dumps," both to bring out different qualities in the chiles and to avoid undesirable bitter flavors that develop when some spices, like cumin, are cooked for too long. A proper Texas chili will have a complex, layered flavor, with a sauce that's thick and red and coats tender bits of beef like paint.

Serves 6 to 8

For the beef

2 tablespoons bacon grease or shortening

2 ancho chiles, stems and seeds removed

2 guajillo chiles, stems and seeds removed

4 cascabel chiles, stems and seeds removed

4 pounds coarse-ground chili beef or stew meat, cut into ½-inch dice (see Note)

Salt and ground black pepper

1 quart beef stock

1 quart chicken stock

1 (8-ounce) can tomato sauce

For the 2-hour spice dump

1 tablespoon onion powder

1 tablespoon granulated garlic

1 tablespoon paprika

1 tablespoon Texas-style chili powder

2 teaspoons ground New Mexico chile

1 teaspoon jalapeño chile powder

1 teaspoon cayenne pepper

For the 15-minute spice dump

2 tablespoons Texas-style chili powder

1 tablespoon ground cumin

1 tablespoon brown sugar

1 tablespoon red wine vinegar

Salt and ground black pepper

Melt the bacon grease over medium heat in a large, heavy-bottomed pot or Dutch oven. Toast the dried chiles in the grease until they become fragrant and begin to puff. Add to a blender with enough boiling water just to cover. Let sit while you brown the meat.

Working in batches, brown the meat in the same pot over medium-high heat, adding a large pinch of salt and pepper to each batch.

Return all the meat to the pan and add the stocks and tomato sauce, stirring to combine while scraping up any browned bits stuck to the bottom of the pot. Bring to a boil.

Blend the chiles until smooth. Add the chile puree to the meat, stir to combine, and cook uncovered, at a simmer, for about 2 hours, stirring occasionally.

After 2 hours, add all the ingredients for the 2-hour spice dump.

Cook for 1 hour; the chili should be just slightly looser than you want the final dish to be.

Add all the ingredients for the 15-minute spice dump; cook for 15 more minutes. Taste for seasoning and serve.

Note: Freezing the meat for 20 minutes will make it easier to dice.

To Bean or Not to Bean

If you are reading this, the world must not have come to an end after all. I am especially relieved. Because if the final ruination of all mankind had occurred, it would have been yours truly who would have been blamed. See, curiosity recently got the best of me, and I did one of the most unspeakably un-Texan things a Texan could ever do. I made a big ol' pot of chili. With beans.

Don't try to tell me you haven't wondered what would happen yourself. Every Texan has had the no-beans-in-chili mantra so thoroughly drilled into him that we presume, en masse, to have been born with the knowledge that chili, at least Texas chili, or *real* chili, as it is referred to around these parts, includes nary one bean among its ingredients. Ever. But why is this? And what happens when it does?

Chili con carne originated in Texas and is, to the disappointment of barbecue enthusiasts everywhere, the official state dish. Indeed, steaming bowls of red were being served on the plazas of old San Antonio way back in the nineteenth century by women we've come to know as the Chili Queens. The historical record tells us that these maiden chilis didn't have beans. Thus, neither have subsequent batches. But the resolution dubbing chili our state dish, which gives a nod to the Queens, did not codify any specific recipe, or even make mention of beans at all. The fact is, unless you're a contestant in a cookoff, where beans are considered "filler" and are strongly frowned upon, there exists no official ban on beans.

The recipe I've used for decades is a hybrid, based partly on that of famed Dallas newspaperman and chili buff Frank X. Tolbert, who penned the seminal chili book *A Bowl of Red* in 1953, and partly on my memory of my dad's unwritten recipe. I break it out about the time of the first cool snap and utilize it throughout the winter. It does not call for beans. And for the record, I had, until this exploratory batch, never once cooked a pot of chili with beans. Ever.

The Texanist is *Texas Monthly* senior editor David Courtney.

So when the idea for this experiment first struck me, I wondered how a person would even undertake such a mixture. I turned to trusted cookbooks for a chili-with-beans recipe, to no avail. A look at the internet offered only strange Midwestern formulas that included beans but also weird components like minced bell pepper and a celery stalk. What are we making here, fajitas and Bloody Marys? I was on my own.

But having been warned against my plan by friends ("Have you lost your mind?"), colleagues ("We're going to get a lot of letters"), culinarians ("The beans will turn to mush"), and my beloved wife ("You're an idiot!"), I was a little worried. Would the beans really turn to mush? My inner gastronome told me to keep it simple, so I decided to go with canned beans, which I would add late in the process, hoping they would hold their form.

My trip to the grocery store was fraught. As I filled my basket with three pounds of lean chuck, beef suet, dried anchos, fresh garlic, and cumin seeds (if you don't already toast and crush your own cumin, the Texanist highly recommends that you start), my palms began to sweat. I almost chickened out but then pulled myself together at a tray of cheese samples before pressing onward to the beans. I had settled on pintos, thinking they were a better option than kidney, black, or—yuck—navy. Eden Organic Pinto Beans (no salt added) looked to be a contender. Until, that is, I examined the listed ingredients. Organic pinto beans. Okay. Water. Okay. Kombu seaweed. What the #%*@?! Seaweed, although not as expressly disparaged as the beans themselves, felt like an abomination too far. I went with another high-dollar, low-sodium, no-seaweed brand. And then picked up a box of saltines, an onion, cheddar cheese, and a few fresh jalapeños for garnishment. And a six-pack of Mexican suds to wash it all down.

While cooking, I kept rationalizing to myself that although traditional Texas chili is a simple and unadulterated potion in its preparation, it is very often enhanced post-preparation. See chili dogs, Frito pies, decorated eggs, chili rice, smothered enchiladas, chili-cheese fries, etcetera. I had nothing to apologize for or be ashamed of. But I hesitated when the time came to add the beans. I questioned the whole endeavor. The missus stood over me and chimed in, "You're going to ruin it." Sweat beaded on my forehead. Was I about to wreck a perfectly good pot of chili?

In the end, the chili with beans turned out real nice—with intact beans. I'm not ashamed to say it: This was some good chili.

Adding beans may be disqualifying on the cookoff circuit and distasteful to chili-headed purists, but it turns out that it's not at all as calamitous as you had imagined. The truth is, chili with beans is aromatic, piquant, and delicious, just like chili ought to be.

Lao Texas Chili

This truly remarkable chili comes from chef Donny Sirisavath, of now closed (but perhaps to return in pop-up form!) Khao Noodle Shop, in Dallas. Taking inspiration from Texas chili (ground beef, smoked paprika, cumin) and Laotian soups and stews (lemongrass, galangal, fish sauce), he's created a super-flavorful one-pot dish that combines the best of both cuisines.

Serves 6

2 stalks lemongrass, woody exterior removed, cut into large chunks

1 (3- to 4-inch) piece galangal, peeled and cut into large chunks

2 tablespoons vegetable oil

1 medium yellow onion, diced

2 shallots, finely diced

2 pounds ground beef (chuck or sirloin; see Note)

Salt and ground black pepper

1 poblano chile, stem and seeds removed, diced

3 garlic cloves, minced

1½ teaspoons cayenne pepper

1½ tablespoons smoked paprika

1 to 1½ tablespoons Thai chile flakes (depending on your spice tolerance)

1 tablespoon ground cumin

3 to 4 bai ki hoot (makrut lime leaves)

½ cup water

1 bottle Beerlao or a Mexican lager

2 tomatoes, roasted in a dry pan until blackened, then diced, or one 15.5-ounce can diced roasted tomatoes

1 (6-ounce) can tomato paste

2 tablespoons fish sauce

1 tablespoon sugar

Chopped fresh cilantro, chopped green onion, shredded cheddar cheese, sour cream, diced yellow onion, Thai chile flakes, ground black pepper, and fried shallots or onion, for garnish

In a food processor, process the lemongrass and galangal until thoroughly minced. Set aside.

Heat the oil in a heavy-bottomed pot or Dutch oven over high heat. Add one-quarter of both the onion and the diced shallots, then add the beef. Cook for 2 to 3 minutes, then add some salt and black pepper. Lower the heat to medium and continue to cook, stirring regularly, for 5 to 6 minutes, until the beef is fully cooked. Reduce the heat to medium, then use a slotted spoon to remove the beef mixture to a bowl. Set aside.

Add the remaining onion and shallots and poblano chile to the pot. Cook for 3 to 4 minutes, until the onion is translucent. Add the garlic, cayenne, smoked paprika, chile flakes, cumin, 1 tablespoon black pepper, the lemongrass mixture, and the lime leaves. Stir to combine.

Add the water and half of the beer, and use a spoon to scrape up all the browned bits stuck to the bottom of the pot. Add the roasted tomatoes and tomato paste and bring to a simmer. Simmer for 5 minutes, stirring regularly.

Add the beef and any drippings to the pot, along with the remaining beer. Stir, then add the fish sauce, sugar, and 1 tablespoon salt. Stir and bring to a gentle boil over medium-high heat. Reduce the heat to medium-low and simmer, covered, for another 5 minutes. Stir to make sure nothing has stuck to the bottom of the pot, replace the lid, and simmer for 30 minutes, stirring occasionally.

Remove the lid and let simmer for another 15 minutes, or until thick and saucy. Taste and adjust the seasoning.

Ladle the chili into bowls and garnish to your liking.

Note: If desired, you may also add ½ pound diced flank steak that has been simmered in water for 2 to 3 hours, until tender.

Chile Pequin and Gulf Shrimp Aguachile

Native to the arroyos of South and West Texas, the chile pequin is a tiny chile that packs a punch. Often dried and crushed for seasoning or soaked in vinegar for a simple hot sauce, here these chiles provide flavor and heat to a Gulf shrimp aguachile from chef Alejandro Paredes, of Carnitas Lonja and Fish Lonja, in San Antonio.

Serves 1 to 2

1 small ripe tomato

1 cup fresh lime juice

¼ cup dried chile pequin

¼ cup fresh cilantro leaves

1 pinch dried oregano

Salt

7 to 10 Gulf shrimp (16–20s), peeled and deveined

1 cucumber, sliced

½ avocado, diced

¼ red onion, diced

Heat a small cast-iron skillet over medium heat. Add the tomato and dry-roast until blackened, about 5 minutes on each side. Let cool.

In a blender, combine the tomato, lime juice, chile, cilantro leaves, and oregano. Blend until smooth. Season with salt.

In a large bowl, combine the shrimp with the tomato mixture and let sit for 10 to 15 minutes (make sure it's no more than 25 minutes), until opaque.

Serve on a large plate, with the shrimp drowning in the sauce and garnished with the cucumber, avocado, and onion.

Pickled Jalapeños

Pickling and fermenting are all the rage in the culinary world, but Texans have long known the joys of a peck of pickled peppers. Particularly the jalapeño, about which food writer Alison Cook said in *Texas Monthly* in 1983, "If Texans hold any truth to be self-evident, it is that there is nothing that would not be improved by the addition of a little jalapeño." Pickled, the fiery slivers cut the richness of barbecue, give bean dip a little tang, and steal the limelight atop the stage that is a composed nacho.

Makes about 1 pint

1 pound jalapeño chiles, stems removed, cut into ½-inch-thick slices

1 cup distilled white vinegar

1 cup water

½ cup sugar

2 garlic cloves, peeled

Pinch dried oregano

Put the chile slices in a heat-tolerant glass jar.

Combine the vinegar, water, sugar, garlic, and oregano in a medium pot over medium heat. Bring to a simmer and cook until the sugar is dissolved.

Carefully pour the hot brine over the jalapeños to fully submerge them.

Cover and refrigerate for at least 48 hours before using. These will keep for up to 2 months in the refrigerator (if they last that long).

ODE TO THE
Chile Pequin

When chile peppers are mentioned in Texas, the jalapeño comes first to mind. But this overrated member of the pepper family isn't a native. The true Texas chile, the only one that grows wild in the state, is the fiery chile pequin. Bristling with hundreds of oval pods smaller than the nail on a woman's little finger, the knee-high bushes grow abundantly in open country and backyards from South Texas to South America. Green or red, fresh or dried, the chile is stewed with meat or beans, ground to make salsas, and pickled for pepper vinegar.

What sets the wee chile apart is its legendary heat. Anyone who has endured the eye-watering, nose-running experience of eating one whole would probably just as soon have a cigarette stubbed out on their tongue. An undeclared cult of the awe-inspiring chile has grown up over the years, but it differs from jalapeño mania in the way cane-pole catfishing differs from fly-fishing. Any fool can eat fifty jalapeños or catch a passel of catfish, but it takes a connoisseur to quarter a chile pequin before consuming it on a perfectly fried egg or land a trout on a line as delicate as a spider web.

Chile pequins are still gathered mostly by hand. Some growers are experimenting with planting them, but by and large the harvest is wild. The chile pequin remains as it always has, a chile for the few rather than the many, a chile that can be domesticated but never completely tamed.—*Patricia Sharpe*

Blackberry Cobbler

Come May and June, Texas roadways, ravines, and fence lines erupt in boisterous bushes of sweet, juicy blackberries ripe for the picking. For many Texas families, setting out with coolers and buckets to go berry hunting is a summertime tradition. But if you'd rather not contend with the inevitable thorns and purple-stained fingers, pick up a carton or two at your local farmers market.

Makes 1 (9-inch) pie

For the crust

¾ cup all-purpose flour

½ teaspoon salt

½ teaspoon sugar, plus more for dusting

4 tablespoons (½ stick) cold unsalted butter, cut into small pieces

¼ cup ice water, or more as needed

Milk, for brushing the crust

For the filling

3 tablespoons unsalted butter

3 tablespoons all-purpose flour

1 teaspoon fresh lemon juice

½ teaspoon ground cinnamon

1 cup sugar

½ teaspoon salt

3 cups blackberries (fresh or frozen)

TO MAKE THE CRUST:

Preheat the oven to 450°F.

Whisk together the flour, salt, and sugar in a large bowl. Add the butter and, using a fork or pastry cutter, work it into the flour mixture until crumbly. Sprinkle with the ice water, adding a little at a time and stirring with a spoon, until the crust just comes together.

Form the dough into a ball and, on a lightly floured surface, roll it out into a 14-inch circle. Gently drape the dough over a pie dish, easing it into the bottom and taking care not to tear it. Trim off any excess dough that hangs over the edge of the pie dish and set it aside. Refrigerate the crust while you prepare the rest of the pie.

Combine the dough scraps and roll them out. Use a cookie cutter to cut them into desired shapes. Set these on a parchment-lined plate and refrigerate.

TO MAKE THE FILLING:

Set a small saucepan over medium heat and add the butter. Once the butter melts, whisk in the flour and lemon juice. Remove from the heat.

In a large bowl, stir together the butter mixture, cinnamon, sugar, and salt. Gently stir in the berries until they are fully coated.

Pour the berry mixture into the prepared pie crust and cover with the dough shapes. Brush them with milk and sprinkle lightly with sugar.

Place the pie dish on a cookie sheet. Bake for 10 minutes, or until the edges of the crust start to brown. Cover the edges with foil and lower the oven temperature to 375°F. Bake for another 30 minutes; it should be bubbling but will not set until it cools. Let cool on a wire rack before serving.

Peach Cobbler

Is there anything better than a fresh, peak-season Texas peach? Clearly not—but this cobbler comes pretty close. Taking inspiration from the scoop-and-serve cobblers of barbecue joints and lunch cafeterias across the state, this recipe lets the peaches take center stage, accented with a hint of cinnamon and topped with a simple buttermilk biscuit–like topping.

Makes one 9 x 13-inch pan of cobbler

Unsalted butter, for greasing

For the filling

1 cup sugar

1 teaspoon ground cinnamon

2 tablespoons cornstarch

4 pounds peaches, peeled, pitted, and sliced

Juice of 1 lemon

For the topping

1½ cups all-purpose flour

1 cup sugar

1 tablespoon baking powder

1 teaspoon salt

½ cup (1 stick) cold unsalted butter, diced

1¼ cups buttermilk

TO MAKE THE FILLING:

Preheat the oven to 375°F. Butter a 9 x 13-inch baking dish.

In a large bowl, whisk together the sugar, cinnamon, and cornstarch. Add the peaches and lemon juice, stir to combine, then pour into the prepared baking dish.

TO MAKE THE TOPPING:

In a large bowl, whisk together the dry ingredients. Use a fork or pastry cutter to cut the butter into the flour mixture. Add the buttermilk and stir to combine into a shaggy dough.

Use a large spoon to dollop the topping evenly over the peaches. You can leave them as separate biscuits or use a spatula to smooth the topping more evenly over the fruit.

Place the baking dish on a sheet pan and bake for 1 hour, or until the fruit is bubbling and the topping is golden. Allow to cool for at least 10 minutes before serving; serve warm or at room temperature, with a scoop of vanilla ice cream.

Note: If peaches are out of season, you can use defrosted frozen peach slices. For that real steam-table, cafeteria-style cobbler, substitute shortening for the butter.

Pecan Pie

"Though there are many ways to enjoy pecans, it is practically a given among Texans that they belong, first and foremost, in a pie." So proclaims Senate Concurrent Resolution 12, in which the pecan pie was declared the official pie of Texas. No dessert table is complete without one of these impossibly sweet creations, which usually involve a flaky crust embracing a dense, sugary amber of butter and corn syrup studded with—wouldn't you know it—Texas's official state nut. Which falls, naturally, from our official state tree.

Makes one 9-inch pie

For the crust

1 cup all-purpose flour, plus more for dusting the work surface and rolling pin

1 teaspoon sugar

½ teaspoon salt

6 tablespoons cold unsalted butter, cut into small cubes

¼ cup ice water, or more as needed

For the filling

3 large eggs

⅓ cup sugar

⅓ cup light corn syrup, such as Karo

⅓ cup dark corn syrup, such as Karo

2 tablespoons unsalted butter, melted

1 teaspoon vanilla extract

2½ cups whole pecans (or half or quarter pieces, but not the chopped kind)

TO MAKE THE CRUST:

Preheat the oven to 375°F.

In a large bowl, whisk together the flour, sugar, and salt. Use a pastry cutter or fork to work the butter into the flour mixture until only pea-size pieces of butter remain. Drizzle with ice water a teaspoon or two at a time, stirring between additions. Add water only until the dough just comes together, then work briefly with your hands and shape into a round disk. Wrap in plastic and refrigerate for 20 minutes.

On a floured surface, use a rolling pin to roll out the dough into a 12-inch circle. Carefully move the circle of dough into a 9-inch deep-dish pie plate, taking care to press it into the corners. Roll the edges under themselves and crimp to the edge of the pie plate with a fork. Use the fork to prick the bottom of the crust all over, then line with foil. Add dried beans or pie weights and bake for 15 minutes. Remove from the oven, carefully remove the foil and pie weights, and let cool while you prepare the filling.

TO MAKE THE FILLING:

In a large bowl, beat the eggs, then stir in the sugar, light and dark corn syrups, butter, and vanilla. Mix well. Add 2 cups of the pecans and mix well again.

Pour the mixture into the prepared crust. The surface will have gaps with no pecans. Use the remaining pecans to fill these gaps as needed.

Bake for about 1 hour, until the pie is nearly set but still has some wiggle in the center. Let cool completely

Pralines

Thanks to our plenitude of wild pecans, the praline looms large in Texans' taste memories, that sugary, nutty, creamy-crispy confection without which no No. 1 dinner is complete. As for cooking up a batch, well, pralines are easy to make and easy to mess up. Humidity, timing, temperature—all can conspire against you. When they work, they're sublime; when they don't, you have a seriously good topping for some vanilla ice cream.

Makes about 1 dozen pralines

Nonstick cooking spray

2 cups light brown sugar

¼ cup light corn syrup

¼ cup heavy cream

2 tablespoons unsalted butter

1 teaspoon salt

2 cups pecan halves

2 teaspoons vanilla extract

Line a sheet pan with parchment paper or foil and spray with cooking spray.

In a large saucepan, combine the brown sugar, corn syrup, cream, butter, and salt. Bring to a boil over medium heat and cook, stirring, until the mixture reaches 235°F on a candy thermometer. (This is called the soft-ball stage.) Remove from the heat.

Add the pecans and vanilla and gently stir until the caramel begins to fade from a high, shiny gloss to a dull, more opaque color, 1 to 2 minutes.

Spoon tablespoon-size drops of pralines onto the prepared sheet pan. Let cool completely.

CHAPTER 2

Smoke
Signals

BY DANIEL VAUGHN

Brisket, Beans, and Banana Pudding

You're going to hear a lot about authenticity in any discussion of Texas barbecue. All too common are arguments about which kind of seasoning, cut of meat, species of wood, and type of smoker is the most traditional. I find those debates as fruitless as a dead post oak tree. There is no right answer, because our barbecue culture is constantly evolving. Joints serving only brisket would have seemed strange just sixty years ago; at the turn of this century, finding a place that served smoked beef short ribs would have required quite an effort. Yesterday's innovation is today's tradition.

The trinity of brisket, pork ribs, and sausage is the foundation of the state's modern-day barbecue menu, and there's a recipe for each in this chapter. Of course, none can exactly be considered foolproof. Good barbecue requires practice to master. Just as important as ingredients and methodology are attention to detail, plenty of patience, and sheer dedication. If you've ever served tough ribs, rubbery sausage links, or a brisket so overcooked it turned to mush on your cutting block, then you'll understand. We're happy to get you started on solid footing.

We've tried to strike a balance in this group of recipes between the more traditional (there's that word again) and the innovative. It was important for this collection to reflect how Texans actually eat barbecue today, and that includes using smoked brisket as a building block for spicy guisada (as in the recipe from Zavala's, in Grand Prairie) or as the filling in empanadas (from Austin's beloved Valentina's). A beef rib is great served on the bone, but what about as a carefully constructed bite of nigiri, like they serve at Khói Barbecue, in Houston? Only those who haven't tried it will knock it.

The influences on the state's smoked-meat customs have always been broader than what's reflected in the Central Texas temples of barbecue. Barbacoa de cabeza—a South Texas style that involves cooking whole cow heads in the ground over wood coals—says as much about our barbecue roots as a brisket smoked over oak in Austin. That's why we're excited to share a recipe from Seguin's Burnt Bean Co. for tatema, a derivation of barbacoa that uses beef cheeks rather than the whole head. It is a perfect example of the blending of techniques that is emblematic of modern Texas barbecue.

It wouldn't be barbecue without a few sides, some banana pudding, and yes, even barbecue sauce. We've got those covered. And if this chapter doesn't fully satiate your appetite for smoked meat, don't fret. There are a few appearances from some of your favorite pitmasters throughout the book, so keep searching for more inspiration. Now get that fire lit, and may your smoke always be clean.

Brisket

You could write an entire book on how to smoke brisket perfectly. From wood selection, pit modifications, and fire management to trimming uncooked beef and slicing the thing up when it's done, explicating the minutiae of the most famous cut of meat in Texas could fill volumes. This recipe is not that. What it is, instead, is a road map that will get you most of the way to where you need to go (cue an "I had a truck like that once" joke). The rest of it—the pursuit of that thin blue smoke and perfect pink smoke ring—is mostly practice. We recommend keeping a small notebook to track your smokes: temperature, timing, what worked, what didn't. You'll be the star of your neighborhood backyard barbecue circuit before you know it.

Makes 1 genuine Central Texas–style smoked brisket

1 packer-cut brisket, 14 to 15 pounds

½ cup salt

½ cup coarsely ground black pepper

Special equipment: smoker

Trim the fat on the brisket to about ½ inch. Combine the salt and pepper and generously season the brisket all over. (You may not need all the seasoning—just make sure it's good and covered.) Place the brisket on a sheet pan and refrigerate, covered in foil or plastic, overnight.

The next day, let the brisket come to room temperature. Heat a smoker to 250°F (plus or minus 10). Once you've got the temperature more or less stable, place the brisket directly on the grate with the fat side up.

At this point, leave it alone. The internal temperature of the brisket will rise for a bit and then stop rising—that's the famous "brisket stall." If you like, at this point you can wrap the brisket in foil to speed up the process (although some may consider that cheating).

Cook the brisket until it reaches 202 to 203°F—it should feel tender to the touch, as though the meat has relaxed. At this point, remove it from the smoker, wrap it in butcher paper, and let it rest for about an hour in a cooler. Do not skip this step: it's important for the brisket to rest or it will lose all its juices when you cut into it.

Slice and serve.

Brisket

Why do we love brisket above all other barbecued meats? Is it because of its resonant beefy flavor, its exterior as shiny as black patent leather, its rivulets of fat moistening every mouthful and staining the eater's shirt? Yes. The very nature of brisket is to be delicious. Yet there's more to it than that. We love brisket because cooking it is a spiritual path, a quest that, as a wise man once said, begins with a single log.

The steps toward enlightenment are threefold. The seeker of Brisket Truth must first embrace mental discipline, immersing himself in the craft of tending the fire and minding the meat. Second, the seeker must practice physical discipline, to be capable of wielding and slicing a twelve-pound brisket after having consumed a six-pack of Shiner Bock. Finally, the seeker must exhibit spiritual discipline, neither napping beside the smoker, nor wandering inside to catch the game on TV, nor sneaking off to update his Facebook page. The person who does these things is granted true knowledge of the brisket's essence. He who honors this ritual is prepared for life.—*Patricia Sharpe*

Brisket Guisada

This riff on traditional carne guisada from Zavala's, in Grand Prairie, throws the entire stew—brisket, tomatoes, chiles, and all—into the smoker. It's a little bit barbecue, a little bit Tex-Mex, and magic in a tortilla. The serranos mellow quite a bit as the guisada smokes, but, as pitmaster Joe Zavala says, it should still have a little kick when it's done.

Serves 8 to 10

1 brisket, about 10 pounds, trimmed of fat and cut into ½-inch cubes

2 tablespoons kosher salt

2 tablespoons ground black pepper

4 tomatoes, cored and roughly chopped

4 serrano chiles, stems removed and roughly chopped

3 garlic cloves, peeled

⅓ cup all-purpose flour

Flour tortillas, for serving

Special equipment: smoker

Prepare a smoker to 225°F.

Cover the brisket with the salt and pepper and place in a large disposable foil roasting tray. Smoke, uncovered, for 90 minutes, stirring every 30 minutes or so.

In a medium pot, add the tomatoes, chiles, garlic, and enough water to just cover. Bring to a boil over high heat, then reduce to a simmer and cook for 8 minutes, or until the vegetables have softened. Use an immersion blender to blend until smooth, then whisk in the flour until it is fully incorporated and no lumps remain.

Add the tomato sauce to the brisket and stir to combine. Cover with foil. Cook for 6 to 7 hours, stirring every hour, until the meat is tender. Serve with flour tortillas.

Goldee's House Sausage

Who knew when a group of twentysomething pals—Lane Milne, Jalen Heard, Nupohn Inthanousay, Jonny White, and PJ Inthanousay—took over an abandoned building in Fort Worth shortly before a global pandemic hit that their joint would end up ranked the best in the state by *Texas Monthly*? One of the (many) specialties of the Goldee's house is sausage, and the team often riffs on the theme; take their Laotian beef links, served with sticky rice and tangy jeow som. But this recipe is for a classic Texas-style link touched with a little Goldee's magic, like swapping out the usual chile powder for gochugaru (Korean chile powder). This recipe takes three days to make, so plan ahead.

Makes 5 pounds sausage links

10 to 12 feet sausage casings

3½ pounds lean brisket, fat and silverskin trimmed (see Note)

1½ pounds fat (this can be the fat you trimmed from the brisket, or pork or beef fat purchased from the butcher, or a combination)

2½ tablespoons kosher salt

1 teaspoon pink curing salt

1 tablespoon garlic powder

1 tablespoon onion powder

2 tablespoons gochugaru

2½ tablespoons coarsely ground black pepper

2 tablespoons mustard seeds

1 tablespoon mustard powder

1½ teaspoons dried sage

10 garlic cloves, peeled

½ cup unsalted beef or chicken stock

¾ cup powdered milk

Special equipment: meat grinder, sausage stuffer, smoker

Note: Silverskin is a thin, silvery-gray membrane that covers some cuts of meat. Remove it with a sharp knife before you start cooking.

DAY 1

Rinse the casings thoroughly, taking care to ensure you've washed away all the salt. Place in a sealed container, add enough water to cover, and store overnight in the refrigerator.

Cut the brisket and fat into small cubes. Add the kosher salt, curing salt, garlic powder, onion powder, gochugaru, black pepper, mustard seeds, mustard powder, sage, and garlic. Stir to combine and let sit in the refrigerator overnight.

DAY 2

Drain the casings and cover with fresh water. Let soak in the fresh water for 1 hour before using.

Put the meat mixture in the freezer for 30 minutes before grinding. Then add to the meat grinder slowly until all of it has been processed.

Once the meat is ground, mix together by hand for 1 minute. Then add the stock and powdered milk and stir until the mixture becomes so sticky that a small patty will stick to your hand.

Use a sausage stuffer to stuff the ground meat tightly into the casings; make sure there are no air bubbles. Twist into links as you go. Place the stuffed sausages on a sheet pan and let dry, uncovered, in the refrigerator overnight.

DAY 3

Cut the sausages into separate links. Heat a smoker to between 250 and 275°F. Cook until the sausages reach an internal temperature of 160°F. (If you don't have a smoker, you can roast them in a 350°F oven for 20 to 30 minutes.)

Let the sausages rest for 5 minutes before serving.

Pork Ribs

The key to a great rack of ribs is to take them to just tender; if the meat is falling off the bone, they've cooked for too long. Plenty of folks get fancy with rib rubs, and you can add all kinds of flavorings, from garlic powder to mustard to brown sugar. For this recipe, though, we've kept it simple. Sometimes it's best to let the smoke do the talking.

Serves 2 to 3, depending on the size of the rack

1 tablespoon salt

1 tablespoon ground black pepper

2 teaspoons sweet paprika

1 rack St. Louis–style pork spareribs, 3 to 4 pounds

Special equipment: smoker

Combine the salt, pepper, and paprika in a small bowl. Season the ribs liberally with the mixture, wrap them in plastic, and refrigerate overnight.

The next day, heat a smoker to between 250 and 275°F. Place the ribs directly on the grate, bone-side down, with the thickest end of the ribs pointed toward the firebox.

Cook for 4 to 6 hours, flipping the ribs every hour until the internal temperature reaches 165°F. When the ribs are done, they will flop over a pair of tongs, and the meat should be tender but not falling off the bone.

Wrap the ribs in foil and let rest for 30 minutes, then cut into individual ribs and serve.

Brisket Empanadas

When it comes to uniting barbecue with Latin American flavors, there's no better matchmaker than pitmaster Miguel Vidal, of Valentina's Tex-Mex BBQ, in Austin. If you're lucky enough to find yourself with some leftover brisket, try his take on empanadas. Don't be deterred by the lengthy recipe. These come together easily.

Makes 8 to 10 empanadas

For the dough

2 cups masa harina

1 teaspoon kosher salt

½ teaspoon ground annatto

½ teaspoon ground cumin

½ teaspoon granulated garlic

1¾ cups hot water

For the filling

2 teaspoons salt

½ pound Yukon Gold potatoes, peeled and cut into 1-inch chunks

2 tablespoons olive oil

4 garlic cloves, minced

½ white onion, finely diced

1 pound smoked brisket, chopped (or 1 pound ground beef)

1 teaspoon chili powder

1 teaspoon granulated garlic

1 teaspoon ground annatto

1 teaspoon ground cumin

1 teaspoon ground black pepper

1 teaspoon paprika

For the empanadas

Vegetable oil, for frying

Tomatillo Salsa (page 110)

TO MAKE THE DOUGH:

Combine the masa harina, salt, annatto, cumin, and granulated garlic in a large bowl. Add 1½ cups of the water (the remaining ¼ cup can be added if the dough is too dry). Stir together, then knead the dough until it's smooth and slightly moist (if it's too dry, it will break when you form the empanadas). Place in a resealable plastic bag with the air squeezed out, and set aside while you prepare the filling.

TO MAKE THE FILLING:

In a medium pot, bring about 3 cups water with the salt to a boil. Add the potatoes and boil for 10 minutes, or until cooked through. Drain and set aside.

Heat a cast-iron skillet over medium heat and add the oil. Add the garlic and onion and cook until softened, about 3 minutes. Add the brisket or ground beef and cook, stirring, to break the meat apart until warmed through (if using ground beef, sauté until the meat is cooked, about 6 minutes). Add the chili powder, granulated garlic, annatto, cumin, black pepper, paprika, and potatoes, stirring to break the potatoes up into the filling. Remove from the pan to a large bowl and let cool.

TO MAKE THE EMPANADAS:

Take a golf ball–size piece of the dough and place it between 2 sheets of plastic wrap (or 2 halves of a resealable plastic bag, cut apart). Press the dough ball down until it's about ¼ inch thick and 3 inches in diameter. Gently remove the plastic.

Cradle the dough round in the palm of one hand and use a spoon to add 2 to 3 teaspoons of filling. Pinch the empanada closed, making sure the edges are fully sealed so it doesn't open while cooking.

Heat about 4 inches of oil to 375°F in a large, heavy-bottomed pot and fry the empanadas for 2 minutes, or until golden brown. Use a spider or slotted spoon to remove to a paper towel–lined tray. Serve with tomatillo salsa.

Korean Smoked Beef Ribs

Khói means "smoke" in Vietnamese, and that's the main ingredient at Houston-based Khói Barbecue, where brothers Don and Theo Nguyen celebrate their Texas and Asian heritage with dishes like brisket pho and beef cheek bánh xèo. These smoked beef ribs represent yet another innovative take on tradition. "Traditional Korean kalbi calls for thin slices across the three rib bones," says Don, "but we keep the rack whole during the cooking process, more in line with Texas barbecue technique." The meat, bathed in a marinade inspired by Los Angeles chef Roy Choi, is delicious. And if you're feeling adventurous, the Nguyens have offered their recipe for beef rib nigiri, which takes the succulent meat to a whole other level.

Serves 6 to 8

6 scallions, chopped

1 Asian pear, peeled, cored, and chopped

1 teaspoon fish sauce

½ cup peeled garlic cloves, about 2 heads

1 white onion, chopped

1 cup soy sauce

½ cup fresh orange juice

¼ cup red wine

6 tablespoons toasted sesame oil

½ cup sugar

1 teaspoon ground black pepper

2 teaspoons toasted sesame seeds

1 rack beef short ribs, about 3 pounds

Special equipment: smoker

Combine all the ingredients except the short ribs in a blender and puree.

Place the short ribs in a large container or bowl. Pour the marinade over the ribs, making sure the beef is coated on all sides. Cover and refrigerate overnight.

Heat a smoker to 275°F. Remove the ribs from the container, reserving the marinade. Smoke the beef ribs directly on the grate for 8 to 10 hours, until the internal temperature reaches 198°F. Brush with the marinade every hour.

When the ribs are done, wrap them in butcher paper, set aside to rest for 1 hour, then serve.

Beef Rib Nigiri

For the nikiri sauce

1 cup soy sauce

⅓ cup cooking sake

⅓ cup mirin

2 tablespoons dashi or stock

TO MAKE THE NIKIRI SAUCE:

Combine the soy sauce, sake, mirin, and dashi or stock in a small saucepan over medium-high heat and cook until the mixture boils. Reduce the heat to medium-low and simmer for 1 to 2 minutes, until the sauce thickens. It should be just slightly thinner than honey.

(cont.)

For the sumeshi (sushi rice)

3 cups Japanese short-grain rice

3 cups water

½ teaspoon salt

¾ cup rice wine vinegar

½ cup sugar

1 tablespoon salt

1 piece kombu

For the nigiri

Korean Smoked Beef Ribs (page 55), cut into thin slices against the grain

¼ cup sesame seeds

¼ cup kimchi, thinly sliced

TO MAKE THE RICE:

If you're using a rice cooker, combine the rice, water, and salt and cook on the sushi rice setting. To make the rice on the stovetop, place the rice in a small pot, cover with the water, and add the salt. Set the heat to high and cover with a lid. Once the water is boiling, open the lid slightly, turn the heat down to medium-low, and simmer for 15 to 20 minutes, until the rice is tender.

While the rice cooks, make the sushi vinegar: combine the vinegar, sugar, salt, and kombu in a small saucepan over medium heat. Stir gently to combine and make sure the sugar dissolves, about 2 minutes. Turn off the heat and remove the kombu.

Place the cooked rice in a large bowl. Add the vinegar mixture and mix it in using a rice paddle or a rubber or silicone spatula.

TO CONSTRUCT THE NIGIRI:

Take 3 ounces of rice (roughly the size of an egg yolk) and place it in your palm. Using the fingers of your opposite hand, form the rice into an oblong shape.

Place the rice on a plate and brush with nikiri sauce. Lay one slice of beef on the sauce-brushed rice. Garnish with sesame seeds and a slice of kimchi. Repeat with the rest of the rice, short ribs, sesame seeds, and kimchi.

Barbacoa Estilo Tatema

Burnt Bean Co., in Seguin, took the number four spot on *Texas Monthly*'s 2021 list of the top fifty barbecue joints in the state thanks to its gluttony-inspiring beef ribs, peppery pork chops, and juicy brisket. But just as spectacular is the Sunday breakfast, when Burnt Bean offers dishes like menudo, huevos rancheros, and this tatema-style barbacoa. *Tatema* is a Spanish word with Aztec origins that refers to barbacoa cooked in the ground with wood coals. Pitmasters Ernest Servantes and David Kirkland use beef cheeks (instead of the whole head) and cook the meat low and slow in a smoker until it's rendered into soft strands of well-seasoned beef ready to be folded into a warm tortilla.

Serves 6

For the beef cheeks

2 tablespoons salt

1 tablespoon granulated garlic

1 tablespoon granulated onion

4 pounds beef cheeks (4 to 5 cheeks, depending on size)

½ white onion, chopped

2 quarts beef stock or water, or more, depending on the size of your pan

Special equipment: smoker

To serve

Corn tortillas

Your favorite salsa

Fresh cilantro, chopped

Chopped white onion

Combine the salt, granulated garlic, and granulated onion in a small bowl. Cover the beef cheeks with the mixture.

Heat a smoker to 250°F using either mesquite or post oak. Smoke the beef cheeks directly on the smoker grate for 5 hours.

Remove the meat from the smoker and set it in a foil pan or roasting pan. Sprinkle the chopped onion over the meat. Fill the pan a third of the way with stock or water and cover the pan with foil.

Raise the heat of the smoker to 275°F. Place the pan on the grate and smoke for another 3 hours.

Remove the pan from the smoker and let sit for 30 minutes. Then remove the meat, reserving 1 cup of the liquid, and shred with a fork or your hands. Add the reserved liquid to the meat.

Serve with corn tortillas, salsa, cilantro, and chopped onion.

Vietnamese Smoked Duck Salad

At Xin Chào, in Houston, second-generation Vietnamese Americans Christine Ha and Tony J. Nguyen (pictured on page 43) use local ingredients to put their own spin on family recipes. Chef Ha explains that this salad "is a perfect representation of what Xin Chào is all about: elevated and modern Vietnamese cuisine with a Texas twist." If you don't have a smoker to prepare the duck, you can substitute smoked turkey from your local barbecue joint, or even rotisserie chicken from the grocery store.

Serves 4 to 6

Smoked Duck

8 cups water

½ cup salt, plus more as needed

1 whole duck (about 5 pounds)

4 stalks lemongrass, woody exterior removed, cut into 4-inch pieces

4 ounces ginger, peeled and thickly sliced (about 1 cup)

Ground black pepper

Special equipment: smoker

For the dressing

½ cup sugar

½ cup hot water

⅓ cup fish sauce

1 Fresno chile, stemmed

3 garlic cloves, peeled

1 (3-inch) piece fresh ginger, peeled

Juice of 2 limes

For the salad

1 (5-ounce) package baby arugula

¼ head red cabbage, shredded

¼ cup fresh Thai basil leaves

¼ cup fresh mint leaves

¼ cup fresh cilantro leaves

TO MAKE THE SMOKED DUCK:

The night before smoking, brine the duck: In a large saucepan, bring the water and salt to a simmer and heat until the salt dissolves. Let cool. Place the duck in a large brining bag and add the brine. Refrigerate overnight.

The next day, remove the duck from the brine and pat dry with paper towels. Stuff the duck with the lemongrass and ginger and rub the skin with salt and black pepper.

Heat a smoker (Ha prefers using post oak) to 225°F (plus or minus 10) and smoke the duck for 4 to 6 hours, until the meat reaches 170°F. Allow to cool, then shred the duck meat.

TO MAKE THE DRESSING:

In a small bowl, dissolve the sugar in the hot water and combine with the fish sauce. Set aside. Add the chile, garlic, and ginger to a food processor and process until minced. Add the minced mixture to the fish sauce, then add the lime juice. Stir to combine and set aside.

TO MAKE THE SALAD:

In a large bowl, combine the arugula, cabbage, Thai basil, mint, cilantro, duck, and jackfruit. Add the dressing, a bit at a time, and toss until all the ingredients are generously coated. Place the salad on a large serving platter and garnish with the candied walnuts and fried shallots.

2 cups Smoked Duck meat, cut into bite-size pieces

1 cup jackfruit, cut into matchsticks

½ cup Candied Walnuts (recipe follows)

¼ cup crispy fried shallots

Candied Walnuts

¼ cup sugar

½ cup water

½ teaspoon salt

1 cup walnuts

TO MAKE THE THE CANDIED WALNUTS:

Preheat the oven to 300°F.

In a small saucepan, add all the ingredients and stir to combine. Cook over low heat until the walnuts are glossy and coated, about 10 minutes.

Spread the walnuts on a parchment-lined sheet pan, making sure that they do not touch. Bake for about 20 minutes, until fragrant, taking care not to burn them. Allow to cool completely.

Coleslaw

If you're a serious barbecue fan, you've no doubt been out to Cattleack, the north Dallas joint owned by Todd and Misty David (which ranked number six on *Texas Monthly*'s 2021 list of top fifty barbecue joints). The Davids clearly respect barbecue tradition: they've covered an outside wall with murals of modern pioneers such as Aaron Franklin, Wayne Mueller, and Tootsie Tomanetz. But they're making their own way in the meat world, cooking dishes such as beef bologna, spicy beef boudin, and Wagyu pastrami ribs. And there's no better side than this refreshing, vinegary coleslaw. Todd says it tastes best the day after it's made.

Makes about 6 cups

2½ pounds (about 1 medium head) shredded green cabbage

1 tablespoon salt

1¼ cups apple cider vinegar

1½ cups sugar

1 tablespoon dried yellow mustard

2 tablespoons celery seeds

1 tablespoon ground black pepper

1 tablespoon granulated garlic

⅓ cup canola oil

In a large bowl, stir the cabbage and salt to combine. Set aside while you prepare the dressing.

In a saucepan over low heat, whisk together the vinegar, sugar, mustard, celery seeds, pepper, and granulated garlic. Bring just to a simmer, then remove from the heat (do not boil).

Add the hot dressing to the cabbage and mix well. Allow to sit for 5 minutes, then add the oil and mix thoroughly.

Potato Salad

Mayonnaise, sugar, and vinegar may be the main ingredients of potato salads elsewhere in the country, but if you order a Styrofoam cup of that iconic side at a Texas barbecue joint, you're more likely to get something like this recipe, from *Texas Monthly*'s very own barbecue editor, Daniel Vaughn. Here, yellowy spuds are shot through with tangy dill pickle, the acidity tamed by a dollop of mayonnaise and chunks of creamy egg.

Serves 8 to 10

5 medium russet potatoes (about 2½ pounds), peeled and cubed

½ cup mayonnaise

¼ cup yellow mustard

½ cup dill pickle relish (or finely chopped dill pickles)

2 hard-boiled eggs, peeled and finely chopped

Salt and ground black pepper

Bring a pot of salted water to a boil and add the potatoes; boil for 7 to 8 minutes, until fork tender. Drain and place in a large bowl.

For a creamy-chunky texture, mash the potatoes with a fork, leaving some whole and some just slightly mashed.

In a separate bowl, whisk the mayonnaise, mustard, and relish together for the dressing. Pour the dressing over the potatoes, add in the chopped egg, and mix thoroughly. Season with salt and black pepper.

Smoked Corn Ribs

Potato salad, coleslaw, and pinto beans have long been the foundation of Texas barbecue side offerings. But smoked-meat fans now expect greater variety from the supporting players. Collard greens, mac and cheese, brussels sprouts, and even broccoli salad commonly appear on plates and trays these days. None, though, are as wildly popular as corn, which you can now find served up in nearly every form, including popped. At Nixta, a modernist taco spot on Austin's East Side, chef Edgar Rico has his own take on this popular side, a variation on elotes, one of Mexico's favorite street foods.

Serves 4

4 ears sweet corn, each husked and cut lengthwise into 4 pieces (may be left whole if this proves too difficult)

1 cup (2 sticks) unsalted butter, melted

1 serrano chile

1 tomatillo

2 tablespoons vegetable oil

1½ teaspoons sugar

1½ teaspoons salt

1½ teaspoons white wine vinegar

2 coriander seeds

1 cup mayonnaise

1 cup finely crumbled queso fresco

1 tablespoon chopped fresh chives

1 bunch fresh cilantro, chopped, with a few leaves reserved for garnish

1 lime, cut into wedges

1½ teaspoons gochugaru

Special equipment: smoker

In a large bowl, toss the corn with the melted butter until evenly coated.

In a smoker heated to 225°F with mesquite wood, add the corn, chile, and tomatillo.

After 1 hour of smoking, remove the chile and tomatillo and allow to cool. Leave the corn to smoke for 1 more hour.

Remove the stem from the chile. Add the chile and tomatillo to a blender with the oil, sugar, salt, vinegar, and coriander and blend until smooth. Add the mayonnaise to the mixture and pulse the blender a couple times to combine. Set aside.

Once the corn is finished smoking, toss the pieces in a large bowl with the serrano aioli, half of the queso fresco, the chives, and cilantro.

Place the dressed corn on a platter to serve (chef Rico likes to stack them like a log house). Garnish with the lime wedges, the rest of the queso fresco, some cilantro leaves, and the gochugaru.

Lima Beans with Smoked Pork Neck

Distant Relatives is a barbecue truck in Austin, but there's so much more to it than just smoke and meat: chef Damien Brockway (pictured on page 43) has a background in fine dining, and he opened Distant Relatives to explore the flavors of the African diaspora in the United States. The result is a menu of smoked meats, sandwiches, and seasonal sides—like these lima beans—that includes some of the most creative and delicious offerings you're likely to find anywhere in the state.

Serves 6

1 pound dried lima beans

1 pound smoked pork neck bones (see Note)

1 yellow onion, sliced

4 garlic cloves, sliced

3 jalapeño chiles, stems removed, sliced

2 bay leaves

4 tablespoons (½ stick) cold unsalted butter, cubed

1 teaspoon distilled white vinegar

Cayenne pepper

Ground black pepper

Salt

1 bunch fresh chives, sliced

The day before cooking, in a large bowl, cover the lima beans in 3 quarts cold water and let soak overnight on the counter.

Meanwhile, make the pork neck broth: Place the neck bones, onion, garlic, chiles, and bay leaves in a large pot. Cover with 4 quarts cold water, bring to a gentle simmer, and cook over low heat for 6 hours. Strain the broth and refrigerate it until you're ready to cook the lima beans.

Once the lima beans have soaked, add them to a large pot with the pork broth. Bring to a simmer. Cook over low heat, gently stirring them periodically with a rubber spatula, until the beans are tender but still retain a little bite, 1 to 1½ hours.

When the beans are done, add the butter piece by piece while gently stirring. Once the liquid has reached a glaze-like consistency, add the vinegar. Sprinkle in some cayenne, black pepper, and salt, tasting as you go and adding more to your liking. Garnish with the chives and serve.

Note: Look for smoked pork neck bones in the grocery store near the smoked ham hocks.

Barbecue Sauce

Barbecue sauce is a controversial topic in Texas, with some people eschewing the condiment completely. But if you're going to have sauce with your brisket, it will likely look something like this: tomato-based, with onions, a bit of sweetness, and some sass from Worcestershire and vinegar. You can make this spicier by adding a pinch of cayenne or chipotle powder.

Makes 1 quart

2 tablespoons vegetable oil

½ yellow onion, diced

3 garlic cloves, minced

1 (28-ounce) can crushed tomatoes

½ cup ketchup

½ cup apple cider vinegar

¼ cup light brown sugar

2 tablespoons Worcestershire sauce

1 teaspoon chili powder

1 teaspoon salt

1 teaspoon ground black pepper

½ teaspoon ground cumin

Cayenne pepper or chipotle powder (optional)

Heat a medium saucepan over medium heat and add the oil. Once it's hot, add the onion and cook until softened, about 2 minutes. Add the garlic, stir, and cook for 1 minute more.

Add the rest of the ingredients. Bring to a simmer over medium-low heat. Simmer until the sugar has dissolved and the tomatoes have cooked a bit, about 10 minutes. Stir frequently to prevent splattering. If the sauce is too thick, add a bit of water to thin it, and adjust the seasoning to your taste. (The thickness will vary depending on the brand of crushed tomatoes you use.) For a smoother sauce, use an immersion blender to puree.

Serve warm or at room temperature.

In Defense of Barbecue Sauce

Texans love barbecue sauce. Hell, I love barbecue sauce. Yes, Lockhart's Kreuz Market, once regarded as the Texas barbecue standard-bearer, refused for decades to offer sauce (or forks, for that matter). But that last holdout surrendered four years ago, when it introduced a sauce that's heavy on the Worcestershire and vinegar and lighter on the ketchup than is typical in most Texas sauces. Kreuz's concession, though, hasn't stopped every out-of-state food writer who ever ate a beef rib in Austin during South by Southwest from distilling our barbecue tradition down to one simple adage: "Brisket good, sauce evil."

Well, it's time to set the record straight: it's fine to eat sauce with Texas barbecue.

Maybe you already know this. Maybe you don't need my permission to dunk a slice of brisket into some tangy, viscous goodness. Maybe you're not so much sauce-averse as sauce-hesitant. Maybe you're even sauce-curious. I get it. I prefer mine on the side, lest someone get my preferred ratio of solid to liquid wrong. But I beg you, if there's a squirt bottle on the table, please don't ignore it. Pitmasters are putting much more effort into creating sauces than they used to, and they don't see them as a sop to the undiscerning. Many of them actually love the stuff.

In Austin, miso, serrano, and lime join forces to brighten the burnt ends at Kemuri Tatsu-ya. In Cleburne, Bare Barbecue's Firebox sandwich will have you questioning why it took so long to couple oak-scented brisket with herbaceous chimichurri. And you can thank jalapeño for the bite of the sauce on Slow Bone's Texas Nail sandwich, in Dallas.

Mustard-based sauces are showing up all over Texas. The whole-grain iteration at Houston's Truth Barbeque has become my go-to condiment for just about everything at home. A sweeter version at San Antonio's Smoke Shack BBQ is just as addictive. At Dozier's BBQ, in Fulshear, the mustard sauce hovers at the acidic end of the spectrum, which works well with the juicy sausages.

Some joints have strayed so far from the ordinary that they don't even call their creations barbecue sauce. At Austin's Distant Relatives, the chile-vinegar dip is a rust-red paste of dried Anaheim and African bird chiles mixed with vinegar and aromatics, enriched with butter, and smoked.

None of this is to say that all sauces are good. Sullying a perfectly prepared rib with a tarry mix—likely made with ketchup, corn syrup, and liquid smoke—dredged up from a five-gallon bucket should be a crime, and too many pitmasters are guilty. But there are better choices out there.

Yes, brisket is good. But that doesn't mean that brisket with barbecue sauce is evil. Sometimes the combination is downright delicious. —*Daniel Vaughn*

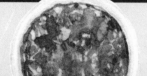

Devil Sauce

Newspaper writer Frank X. Tolbert, best known for his devotion to chili and his classic book on the subject, *A Bowl of Red*, also had another obsession: replicating a particularly spicy barbecue sauce he'd once tasted by a talented cook in East Texas named Will King Solomon. The closest he ever came was a recipe he printed in the *Dallas Morning News* in 1975 by a man named Bill Mitchell. Enter Daniel Vaughn, who set out in 2018 to create this ideal barbecue complement using the building blocks of three recipes: Bill Mitchell's, a traditional sauce diable, and an unconventional recipe from esteemed chef Daniel Boulud (hello, A.1.). The result might not be the "secret devil's sauce" Tolbert long pined for, but it's Daniel's, and that's good enough.

Makes 1 quart

2 cups water

1 small white onion, thinly sliced

4 garlic cloves, peeled and halved

1 (6-ounce) can tomato paste

½ cup apple cider vinegar

¼ cup Worcestershire sauce

¼ cup A.1. Sauce

¼ cup yellow mustard

2 teaspoons hot sauce, such as Tabasco

7 ounces demi-glace (D'Artagnan makes a good version; beef broth will work in a pinch)

Juice of ½ lemon

½ cup dark brown sugar

2 tablespoons kosher salt

2 tablespoons chili powder

1 tablespoon paprika

1 teaspoon ground black pepper

1 teaspoon cayenne pepper

In a medium saucepan, boil the water, onion, and garlic together until the water is reduced by half. Strain and reserve the liquid. If necessary, add water to the reserved liquid until there's a full cup. Return to the pan.

Add the remaining ingredients, bring to a boil, and boil for 10 to 15 minutes, whisking to combine.

Let cool and pour into a 1-quart jar or other container. Add enough water to make a full quart. Shake to combine. Can be served immediately, but flavors meld best if refrigerated overnight.

Refrigerator Pickles

A slice of white bread, a hunk of cheddar cheese, a few slivers of onion—they're all part of the barbecue entourage, little bites meant to complement (and offset) the rich, salty, fatty goodness of smoked meat. But there's no pairing quite like a hunk of beef or pork and a slice of tangy, crunchy dill pickle. Here's a recipe from our own David Courtney, aka the Texanist.

Makes 16 to 20 pickles

2 pounds small unwaxed pickling cucumbers

1 pinch alum powder (optional, for crunchier pickles)

1 garlic clove, peeled

1 hot red chile, or 1 teaspoon chile pequins

1 large sprig fresh dill

½ teaspoon whole allspice

½ teaspoon black peppercorns

4 cups water

2 cups distilled white vinegar

¾ cup canning salt

Place the cucumbers in a large jar or container with a lid and add the alum, if desired, the garlic, red chile, dill, allspice, and peppercorns.

In a large pot, heat the water, vinegar, and salt over medium heat until the salt is dissolved. Pour the hot liquid over the cucumbers until completely submerged. (Add more water to cover the cucumbers if necessary.)

Cover and refrigerate for at least 48 hours before eating.

Banana Pudding

After sampling more than a hundred banana puddings at more than a hundred barbecue joints, Daniel Vaughn decided it was high time to come up with his own recipe for the ultimate post-brisket dessert. Nine batches later, this is where he arrived. His takeaways for the home cook? Sour cream works great for a little acidic zing; Nilla Wafers are just as good as homemade; and skip any and all frozen whipped topping.

Makes one 9 x 13-inch baking dish

6 just-ripe bananas (reserve 4 to make the pudding)

Juice of ¼ lime or lemon

4 cups half-and-half

4 egg yolks

⅓ cup all-purpose flour

½ cup sugar

1 teaspoon kosher salt

2 teaspoons vanilla extract

⅓ cup sour cream

½ box Nilla Wafers (5.5 ounces)

Peel and quarter 2 of the bananas, place in a microwave-safe bowl, and microwave on high for 45 to 60 seconds, until very soft. Mash together with the lime or lemon juice. Add the half-and-half and egg yolks and beat until combined.

Boil a little water in a medium saucepan (to be used as a double boiler). Whisk together the flour, sugar, and salt in a metal bowl that will fit comfortably over the saucepan without touching the water.

Once the water is boiling, place the bowl of dry ingredients on top of the saucepan. Add the banana mixture and whisk continuously for 7 to 10 minutes, until it thickens into something resembling cake batter.

Remove from the heat. Add vanilla and sour cream and stir to combine. Let the mixture cool to room temperature, about 1 hour (if you prefer mushy wafers in the finished product, skip the cooling step and just build the pudding).

Slice the 4 remaining bananas. Layer one-third of the Nilla Wafers on the bottom of a large bowl. Layer half of the bananas over the wafers. Pour half of the pudding mixture over the wafers and bananas. Add another layer with another one-third of the Nilla Wafers and the rest of the sliced bananas. Add the remaining pudding and top with a layer of the remaining Nilla Wafers. Cover and chill in the refrigerator for several hours (or overnight) until completely cool, before serving.

CHAPTER 3

Con Todo

BY JOSÉ R. RALAT

Beyond the
No. 1 Dinner

What's better than a handmade flour tortilla, hot off the comal and slathered with butter? Fluffy, chewy, maybe a tad dusty from the flour used to roll out the dough, the snack might evoke fond memories of family meals in your abuelita's kitchen or festive dinners at one of our state's iconic Mexican restaurants. Again, what's better than that? Not much.

Except maybe that same tortilla served as a taco stuffed with, say, fluffy scrambled eggs and machaca. Or beer-battered fish with a bright cabbage slaw. Or savory ground beef with an avalanche of yellow cheese. Wrapped in foil, nestled in a plastic basket, atop a classic Tex-Mex combination plate—tacos are a ubiquitous part of life in Texas. They are served in gas stations and four-star restaurants, roving trucks and parked trailers, underground pop-ups and wherever a grill or flattop can be accommodated. When Texans are late to their offices, they pick up breakfast tacos en route as edible mea culpas.

But there is more to life than tacos. There is the entire canon of Mexican dishes, many of which we have embraced as our own ever since Texas was Tejas. Mexican food is our foundational cuisine. Without it, we wouldn't have chili, sold in the plazas of San Antonio in the early 1800s by female entrepreneurs who came to be known as Chili Queens. Nor queso, which evolved from queso fundido, a dish of molten cheese garnished with items like mushrooms and chorizo and served with tortillas. We wouldn't have barbecue as we know it (*barbecue* is the literal English translation of the Spanish word *barbacoa*). If not for picadillo, we wouldn't have our version of taco meat. Tamales, those staples of family celebrations, wouldn't be part of our repertoire, nor

the pilgrimage-worthy San Antonio–style puffy taco. And we wouldn't have the pinnacle of our regional Mexican food, cheese enchiladas smothered in hearty, heartwarming chili con carne (and let's not forget the green pepper–bathed platters of far West Texas).

Traditionally called Tex-Mex, our version of Mexican food is as distinctive as any other, like Oaxacan or Sonoran, and equally dynamic. Its ongoing evolution has played out in exciting ways in this past decade, thanks to population shifts and growing awareness of the vastness of Mexican cuisine. Salsa verde and salsa roja remain culinary stalwarts, but they now share menu real estate with fiery, nutty, oil-based salsa macha, which has its origins in Veracruz. Refried and pinto beans have been joined by soupy charro beans. Vegetarian and vegan options, more prevalent in certain regions of Mexico, have also gained a foothold here.

Tortillerias, longtime fixtures of Texas's larger cities, are shining a light on nixtamalization, the ancient practice of cooking and soaking corn kernels in an alkaline solution, which releases essential nutrients from the corn and allows for easier grinding of the grain into masa. Restaurants have taken notice too. Some of our finer establishments have begun serving their own nixtamalized corn tortillas, to be filled or topped with high-quality ingredients worthy of the effort.

Few Texans allow a week to go by without eating some form of Mexican food, be it a handful of tortilla chips, a breakfast taco, a combination platter, or a bowl of red. And since making these dishes yourself is immensely satisfying, we hope these recipes make their way into regular rotation at your house.

Tex-Mex Cheese Enchiladas

We Texans love our enchiladas. And though the varieties are endless, we particularly love the hearty simplicity of a too-hot, brown-and-yellow-painted plate of fragrant corn tortillas rolled around gooey melted cheese, lavished with a meaty "gravy," and sprinkled with tiny toothsome cubes of white onion.

Makes one 9 x 13-inch pan (12 enchiladas)

For the sauce

½ pound ground beef

½ white onion, finely chopped

2 tablespoons all-purpose flour

2 tablespoons chili powder

1 tablespoon paprika

2 teaspoons granulated garlic

1 teaspoon ground cumin

1 teaspoon ground black pepper

2 teaspoons salt

For the enchiladas

Nonstick cooking spray

12 corn tortillas

1 pound shredded mild cheddar or Colby cheese

2 tablespoons finely chopped white onion (optional)

TO MAKE THE SAUCE:

In a large heavy-bottomed pot, cook the ground beef over medium heat, stirring to break up the meat. Once the pink has disappeared, add the onion and cook, stirring, until the onion is translucent, about 3 minutes.

Add the flour, chili powder, paprika, granulated garlic, cumin, black pepper, and salt to the beef and stir. Add 4 cups water, bring to a boil, and reduce the heat to low. Simmer, uncovered, for 45 minutes.

TO ASSEMBLE AND BAKE THE ENCHILADAS:

Preheat the oven to 375°F.

Spray a 9 x 13-inch baking pan with cooking spray. Ladle a large spoonful of the still-warm meat sauce in the bottom of the pan. One at a time, carefully dip each tortilla in the remaining sauce in the pot, then place on a plate. Place about ¼ cup shredded cheese in a line down the center of the tortilla, roll it up, and put it in the baking pan seam-side down. When all the enchiladas have been rolled, cover them with another ladle or two of sauce, and then sprinkle with the remaining cheese.

Bake until the cheese on top is melted and the sauce is bubbling, about 12 minutes. Sprinkle with the onions, if desired, and serve.

Stacked Carnitas Enchiladas with Tomatillo Sauce

At Beto & Son, in Dallas, longtime chef Beto Rodarte and his son Julian team up to create what they call next-generation Mexican food, using fresh, local ingredients to riff on the classics. These are Julian's enchiladas, which he likes to stack instead of roll, a move that makes them both easier to make *and* more attractive on the plate. He serves them with a watermelon radish slaw, sliced avocado, and queso fresco.

Serves 6

For the tomatillo sauce

1 tablespoon olive oil

2 serrano chiles, stems removed, chopped

1 yellow onion, diced

4 garlic cloves, minced

2 (11-ounce) cans tomatillos, drained

1 (10-ounce) can tomatoes with green chiles, such as Ro-Tel

2 tablespoons chicken bouillon, such as Knorr

2 teaspoons salt

1 teaspoon ground cumin

¼ cup chopped fresh cilantro

For the enchiladas

Cooking spray

18 corn tortillas

6 cups Roasted Pork Carnitas (page 96), torn into bite-size pieces (but not entirely shredded)

6 cups Tomatillo Sauce (see above)

1½ cups shredded Oaxaca cheese

Thinly sliced watermelon radish, sliced avocado, and crumbled queso fresco, for serving

TO MAKE THE TOMATILLO SAUCE:

In a large saucepan, heat the oil over medium heat, add the chiles, onion, and garlic, and cook for 2 minutes. Add the tomatillos, tomatoes with green chiles, chicken bouillon, salt, and cumin. Stir to combine and cook for 10 minutes.

Remove the sauce from the heat, add the cilantro, and stir to combine. Use an immersion blender to slightly puree the sauce (you don't want it totally smooth). If the sauce is too thick, add a bit of water and taste once more for seasoning.

TO ASSEMBLE AND COOK THE ENCHILADAS:

Preheat the oven to 375°F.

Spray a sheet pan with cooking spray. Place 1 corn tortilla on the tray. Spread a spoonful of sauce over the tortilla, followed by ½ cup carnitas, followed by 2 tablespoons cheese, and another spoonful of the sauce. Place a second corn tortilla on top and repeat the process. End with the last tortilla and another spoonful of the sauce. (Repeat to make a stack for each serving.)

Place in the oven and bake for 15 minutes, or until the sauce is bubbling and the cheese is melted.

Use a thin metal spatula to lift each tortilla off the pan and onto a serving plate. Garnish with a few slices of watermelon radish, a few slices of avocado, and queso fresco.

Frijoles de Olla

A simple, flavorful, long-simmered pot of pinto beans is pure comfort food. Hugo Garcia, of Con Huevos, in San Antonio, likes to make his in a clay pot, but if you don't have one, he says, any pot will do. The key is to cook the beans at a very low temperature and avoid lifting the lid during cooking.

Makes about 6 cups

2 cups dried pinto beans

3 large garlic cloves, peeled

¼ white onion

2 tablespoons olive oil

1 tablespoon salt

Soak the pinto beans in water to cover for 20 to 30 minutes. Drain the beans, add them to a pot, and cover with 6 to 8 cups water. (More water will make a brothier pot of beans.)

Bring the water to a boil and add the remaining ingredients.

Cover the pot with a lid and allow the water to return to a boil. Remove the lid. The beans will rise to the surface in a minute or so; at this point, cover the pot and reduce the heat to low. Cook, without removing the lid, for 45 minutes to 1 hour, until the beans are soft.

Mexican Rice

This lively sidekick is more commonly known in the United States as Spanish rice, for reasons that are unclear (perhaps for a Spanish style of rice cookery? A conflation of language and country?). But arroz rojo ("red rice") is undoubtedly Mexican. Every family has its own recipe, but most involve first toasting the rice in hot fat and then adding the aromatics. When a dish at a Tex-Mex restaurant comes with rice and beans, chances are the rice will look something like this: tinged red with tomato, fragrant with onion and garlic, and hopefully cozied up to a lake of refried beans.

Serves 4

2 tablespoons vegetable oil

1 cup long-grain white rice

½ white onion, finely diced

3 garlic cloves, minced

2 tablespoons tomato paste

2 cups chicken stock or water

1 teaspoon salt

Heat a large pot over medium heat. Add the oil and rice and stir until the rice is slightly toasted, about 2 minutes. Add the onion and garlic and cook, stirring, until softened, about 3 minutes. Add the tomato paste and cook, stirring, for another minute.

Add the stock or water and salt and bring to a boil. Reduce the heat to low, cover, and cook for 15 to 17 minutes, until the rice is tender. Fluff with a fork and serve.

Chicken Pozole Verde

Round about the time of year when temperatures start to fall, Texans start fantasizing about big ol' pots bubbling away on the stove, giving off aromas that evoke warm, fuzzy feelings of comfort. To that end we turn to pozole, a treasured Mexican dish at the heart of many a Texan's wintertime festivities. Restaurateur Josefina Howard, who introduced New Yorkers to regional Mexican cuisine with her Rosa Mexicano restaurant, once wrote of hearing the earthy stew referred to as "one of the great dishes of international gastronomy, comparable to cassoulet [and] bouillabaisse." This version, which comes together in a snap, is from chef Anastacia Quiñones-Pittman (pictured on page 79), of Dallas's José.

Serves 8

7 cups chicken stock

2 cups water

4 boneless, skinless chicken breasts

1 pound tomatillos, husked and halved

1 small white onion, cut in half

2 poblano chiles, stems and seeds removed

2 jalapeño chiles, stems and seeds removed, halved

4 garlic cloves, smashed

1 bunch fresh cilantro, chopped

1 tablespoon dried oregano

½ teaspoon salt, plus more to taste

2 tablespoons vegetable oil

1 (15.5-ounce) can hominy, drained

Garnishes: shredded cabbage, thinly sliced radishes, thinly sliced onion, sliced avocado, sliced jalapeños, and lime wedges

In a large pot, bring the chicken stock and water to a boil over high heat. Add the chicken breasts, cover, and simmer over very low heat until they're tender and cooked through, about 30 minutes.

Transfer the chicken breasts to a plate and shred the meat. Reserve the cooking liquid (skim any fat from the surface).

In a blender, combine the halved tomatillos, onion, poblano and jalapeño chiles, smashed garlic, chopped cilantro, and oregano. Pulse until coarsely chopped. With the machine on, add 1 cup of the cooking liquid and puree until smooth. Add the salt.

In a large, deep skillet, heat the oil until shimmering. Add the tomatillo puree and cook over medium heat, stirring occasionally, until the sauce turns a deep green, about 12 minutes. Carefully pour the green sauce into the cooking liquid in the pot. Add the hominy and bring to a simmer over medium heat. Add the shredded chicken to the stew, season with salt, and cook until just heated through.

Serve the pozole in deep bowls and allow guests to garnish with cabbage, radishes, onion, avocado, jalapeños, and lime wedges at the table.

Fideo Loco

Fideo loco is an amped-up version of sopa de fideo, a Mexican noodle soup that features thin matchsticks of vermicelli-style pasta toasted in oil and cooked in a tangy tomato broth. The "loco" rendition goes "crazy" with additional ingredients, like meat, beans, and vegetables like potatoes and corn. The dish is an art form in San Antonio, where Hugo Garcia, the chef at Con Huevos, makes it with equal parts sopa de fideo, Frijoles de Olla (page 84), and Beef Picadillo con Papas (page 95). Feel free to add a garnish of fresh cilantro leaves, a squeeze of lime, and *un poco salsa* (Salsa Verde, page 111). The restaurant offers a few additional garnishes: avocado, queso fresco, Oaxaca cheese, and, of course, a corn or flour tortilla on the side.

Serves 6

For the sopa de fideo

¼ cup olive oil

1 (7.5-ounce) bag vermicelli noodles, such as La Moderna

¼ white onion, thinly sliced

½ celery stalk, chopped

½ tomato, thinly sliced

1 (7.4-ounce) can tomato sauce with spices, such as Del Fuerte

1 tablespoon chicken bouillon, such as Knorr

1 tablespoon Knorr Caldo de Tomate (tomato bouillon with chicken flavor)

1½ teaspoons granulated garlic

5 to 8 sprigs cilantro

For the fideo loco

1 recipe Sopa de Fideo

2 cups Frijoles de Olla (page 84), warm

2 cups Beef Picadillo con Papas (page 95), warm

For serving

1 avocado, diced

½ cup crumbled queso fresco

½ cup shredded Oaxaca cheese

1 lime, cut into wedges

¼ cup chopped fresh cilantro

½ cup salsa of your choice

Corn or flour tortillas

TO MAKE THE SOPA DE FIDEO:

Bring 2 quarts water to a boil in a medium pot.

Meanwhile, heat a large soup pot over medium-high heat and add the oil. Once the oil is hot, add the noodles. Stirring continuously, cook until the noodles are golden brown, taking care not to burn them, about 3 minutes.

Once the noodles are toasted, add the onion and cook for 2 to 3 minutes, stirring continuously, until fragrant. Add the boiling water to the pot and stir.

Add the celery, tomato, tomato sauce, chicken bouillon, tomato bouillon, and granulated garlic. Stir, cover with a lid, and bring to a boil. Cook until the noodles are done (be careful not to overcook them).

Add the cilantro and turn the heat off. Cover the pot and let the soup sit for a few minutes before serving.

TO ASSEMBLE THE FIDEO LOCO:

To serve, divide the soup among serving bowls. Add a scoop of the frijoles de olla and the picadillo con papas to each bowl. Garnish as desired with avocado, cheese, lime wedges, cilantro, and salsa, and serve with tortillas on the side.

A Harlingen Native Attempts to Recreate His Family's Fideo

To make a good fideo, you need three things: meat, a molcajete, and vermicelli noodles. In Harlingen, where I grew up, the preferred option was bone-in chicken legs, salted and fried in a pan shimmering with hot oil, just enough so that the skin was crackling and sticky and the juices were runny. In the summer heat, with a chorus of cicadas humming in the chinaberry trees, my mother would smash a garlic clove with a handful of cumin seeds and black peppercorns with the mortar of her mother's molcajete to make the paste from which the fideo would absorb its flavor, like a blooming rose. She'd fry a big Spanish onion in a smattering of chicken grease and swish in the paste. It would sizzle in the pan, and soon enough the kitchen would smell fragrant, exotic, a perfume unlike anything else in the bright, white-hot world of high grasses I grew up in.

Fideo is the simplest of all Tex-Mex dishes: a protein served with heavily seasoned, dry-fried vermicelli noodles. In the communities of South Texas, fideo is synonymous with the boredom of summertime. It's a dish you eat at lunch in the hot blue noons of a Texan summer, your hands sticky with the velouté-like sauce of tomato, pepper, cumin, and garlic, the slinky, thin, dry-fried noodles plump with sauce and begging to be spooned into a corn tortilla. I never saw it made anywhere but in people's houses—nobody I knew brought it to church suppers or barbecues or birthday parties. Fideo is a dish to be savored only in the sumptuous privacy of one's home.

I knew fideo was coming when the kitchen smelled of cumin and garlic. Mom would ask me to get the tortillas. I would pull myself away from my book of saints' lives or, in the summer of 1995, the O.J. Simpson trial, and head down F Street in Harlingen to Tortillería Las Güeras to pick up a pack of freshly made corn tortillas. As I walked home in triple-digit heat, I would hold the paper bag close to me, anticipating the magnificent moment when I could open it and inhale a cloud of hot steam rich with the scent of masa harina—the tortillas, you see, were solely for the fideo, and nothing else. That afternoon, we would eat fideo with corn tortillas on flat Corningware plates with the same ditsy pattern, served with a can of Ranch Style beans. My grandfather would fish out a pickled jalapeño from a jar and squeeze the juice over the entire dish. Best accompanied by reruns of old films on Mexican TV, the dish was a gateway drug of Mexican cuisine. No one else could own it: New Mexicans had their chimichangas and Christmas chili, San Antonians had their enchiladas suizas, but fideo was all South Texas, as authentic as a heat stroke at South Padre Island.

But now I live in Portland, Oregon, and making fideo is not as easy as it was. When I can find it here, hipsters have fancified it with braised beef, with wasabi, with corn smuts from central Mexico called huitlacoches. But for the real thing, you can't overcomplicate fideo. So, after a rough day at work, hankering for a consoling meal from home, I set out to make it myself, nearly ten years since I'd eaten the dish.

First, I had to find the vermicelli. I needed authentic noodles to make the quintessential fideo: Q&Q, with its bright yellow box, its midcentury stylings, and its haystack of noodles. I looked for it everywhere in Portland, far from the reliable H-E-B in Harlingen: in a Whole Foods teeming with urban elites, in a Safeway among jars of chicken tikka masala sauce and Korean kalbi marinade. I took a train out about ten miles east from downtown Portland, and in a small market in a strip mall, I found one solitary box of fideo noodles. The lady working the counter, who had recently arrived from Mexico, asked me if I knew how to make fideo. I said yes, and then she added, almost without delay, "But you have to learn not to undercook the noodles, okay?"

"It's true, mijito, you have to make sure you cook the noodles right or else they'll turn out mushy," my mom said to me that evening. You can't undercook them or overcook them, she continued. Instead you watch for the telltale colorations to appear. The strands of noodles change from blond to brunette in gradations; what you have left is a perfumed, ombré dream.

I had called her on FaceTime, and over video streaming from the very same home where she and I grew up—the same house my great-grandfather and grandfather had died in, one of the first houses in our neighborhood— Mom gently guided me through the recipe her mother had passed down to her. I followed her instructions carefully: the onion must be panfried to translucency, the spices finely ground into a paste mixed with water, and the meat must be cooked first, lest it overcook the noodles. As the cloud of spice paste filled my cold little Oregon kitchen with familiar warmth, I remembered the light and dust of the South Texas I knew: the humidity, the smell of the inky sea breeze that turned a still, hot Harlingen afternoon into a luscious, rainy paradise. I tasted the fideo that was served to my late grandfather while he watched reruns of *Jerry Springer*, the fideo that was served the day of the Reagan funeral, the meager fideo I made with nearly expired boxes of Q&Q during the passage of Hurricane Dolly. The dinner was almost always satisfying, almost always consoling.

It takes vigilance and care to make sure this very simple dish of the Tejano people doesn't turn out to be a grand disappointment. Like all great homemade dishes, fideo transforms simple ingredients into a resplendent complex involuntary memory, triggered by the dry-frying, the sizzle of the water added to the pan, the simmering, the seasoning. The fragrant steam arising from fideo offers glimpses of the dish's origins: the cumin from India, the onion fields, the chiles from Durango or Sinaloa, the carnicero's cuts of beef or chicken, the shack on the South Texas plain where it was first served to families returning from the fields in the humid, oppressive evening. To make fideo is to conjure up these worlds again, and to eat it is to relive, in some tangible way, the gentle comforts of home and history.
—*Joe Galván*

Puffy Tacos

A puffy taco is distinguished by its tortilla: a round of uncooked masa that bobs in hot oil until the moisture evaporates and air pockets form. Plentiful are the purveyors of puffy tacos in San Antonio, which claims unequivocal dominion over this Texas treasure. There's no agreement as to who served it first, and it must be noted that Mexico has no lack of chubby-tortilla delicacies (see: salbutes, gorditas, etcetera). But it is safe to say that a puffy taco from the Alamo City is a work of art, the quick-fried tortilla a consummate expression of fresh masa. This recipe is a primer in the tortilla part. As for fillings, the combination of seasoned ground beef, fresh lettuce, and shredded cheese is traditional, but feel free to experiment.

Masa (see Note)

Canola oil, for frying

TO MAKE THE TORTILLA:

Take a chunk of masa and roll it into a golf ball–size ball. Line the bottom of a tortilla press with some thin, slick plastic (swipe a few pieces from a package of store-bought flour tortillas or cut some circles from a grocery bag), then place the ball on top, a little off center toward the hinges. Cover with another piece of plastic and press out the tortilla. Remove the top sheet, then turn the tortilla over on your palm and peel off the bottom sheet.

THE FRYING:

Heat about 3 inches of canola oil in a cast-iron pot to 375°F. (There's a fine line between puffy and grease-sodden; the temperature of the oil is important, so use a thermometer.) Place the tortilla in the oil; when it rises to the surface and starts to bubble up, use a spatula to press down in the middle of it, forming a gentle U-shaped crease. Let it fry for about 45 seconds more, then remove the tortilla, fill it up, and serve immediately.

Note: Unless you have mad masa skills and plan to nixtamal-ize your own corn, buy fresh masa from a tortilleria. Masa harina (see page 52) is fine, but you won't get that great corny flavor and texture.

Beef Picadillo con Papas

At Con Huevos, in San Antonio, Hugo Garcia cooks his family's recipes, and this flavorful combination of ground beef and potatoes is no exception. The picadillo is perfectly at home in a bowl, but Garcia likes to serve it as the Sonia, a taco named after his mother, with toppings of lettuce, tomato, and crema. It's also one part of the trinity that makes up his Fideo Loco (page 89), which combines equal portions picadillo, beans (page 84), and the tomato-based vermicelli dish called fideo.

Serves 6

2½ pounds ground beef

3 tablespoons Bolner's Fiesta Brand Fajita Seasoning (or make your own, with 1 tablespoon each ground black pepper, onion powder, and garlic powder)

1 white onion, finely diced

4 medium Yukon Gold potatoes, peeled and diced

1 medium tomato, finely diced

1 small jalapeño chile, stem and seeds removed, minced

2 garlic cloves, peeled

½ celery stalk

1 small bunch cilantro

3 tablespoons Knorr Chicken Flavor Bouillon

1 (7.4 ounce) package Del Fuerte Tomato Sauce Seasoned with Spices

Cook the beef in a large, heavy-bottomed pot over medium-high heat, breaking it up with a wooden spoon. Once the meat begins to brown, add the fajita seasoning.

When the meat is thoroughly cooked, add the onion and potatoes. Cook, stirring, for 10 minutes, then add the tomato and chile and cook for another 10 minutes.

While the meat mixture is cooking, combine the garlic, celery, cilantro, bouillon, and tomato sauce in a blender and puree (if the mixture seems too thick, add a little water).

Add the puree to the picadillo and cook over medium heat for 5 minutes, or until the potatoes are tender.

Roasted Pork Carnitas

A simple preparation, this carnitas recipe from Beto & Son, in Dallas, is destined to be layered between corn tortillas and slathered in a bright tomatillo sauce for chef Julian Rodarte's stacked enchiladas (page 83). They'd be just as good in a taco, though, after a brief crisping in a skillet or under a broiler. Since they freeze like a dream, it might be worth making a double batch so you can have it both ways.

Serves 6

3 to 4 pounds pork shoulder, trimmed of fat and cut into 2-inch cubes

1 tablespoon salt

2 teaspoons ground white pepper

1 cup orange juice

Preheat the oven to 350°F.

Place the pork in a roasting pan and add the salt and pepper. Mix with your hands to make sure the seasoning is evenly distributed.

Add the orange juice to the pan, then add as much water as needed to bring the liquid to a level halfway up the pan.

Cover with foil and roast for 2 hours, or until the meat is fork-tender. Remove the foil and roast for another 30 minutes.

Cochinita Pibil

Ninfa's, in Houston, is an institution for many reasons, not least being "Mama" Ninfa Laurenzo, who in 1973 introduced fajitas and tacos al carbón to diners who knew no more of Mexican food than yellow-cheese-smothered combination plates. Years later, Ninfa's continues to celebrate the bright, complex flavors of regional Mexican cuisines, like this Yucatecan dish of achiote-rubbed pork roasted in a banana leaf. Executive chef Alex Padilla says the restaurant serves it with pickled red onions, sour cream, tortillas, and fried plantains, which, he says, you can buy in the freezer section of the grocery store and quickly make at home.

Serves 8

¼ cup salt

¼ cup ground black pepper

2 tablespoons ground cumin

1 cup (8 ounces) achiote paste

Juice of 1 grapefruit

Juice of 3 limes

Juice of 3 lemons

1 (4- to 5-pound) pork butt, cut into 3- to 4-inch chunks

2 medium tomatoes

¼ cup peeled garlic cloves

1½ cups pineapple juice

1 yellow onion, cut into quarters

½ cup red wine vinegar

¼ cup dried oregano

2 tablespoons vegetable oil (if cooking in a skillet)

2 banana leaves

2 bay leaves

In a medium bowl, whisk together the salt, pepper, cumin, achiote, grapefruit juice, lime juice, and lemon juice to make a paste. Place the pork in a shallow dish, rub the paste all over, cover with plastic wrap, and let marinate in the refrigerator overnight.

Preheat the oven to 350°F.

In a medium cast-iron skillet over medium-high heat, roast the tomatoes until charred and softened, flipping with a pair of tongs to make sure all sides are cooked. Remove to a blender. Do the same with the garlic, removing it when brown spots appear.

To the tomato and garlic, add the pineapple juice, onion, vinegar, and oregano and blend until smooth.

If desired, grill the pork briefly over high heat (that's what they do at the restaurant to get a bit of char on it) until marked on all sides, or sear in the vegetable oil in a hot skillet until browned on all sides.

Place the banana leaves in the bottom of a large, heavy-bottomed pot that can go in the oven. Add the meat and cover with the puree; stir to coat the meat. Add the bay leaves, cover, and cook in the oven for 2 hours and 45 minutes to 3 hours, until the meat is tender.

Set the oven to broil. Remove the pork from the braising liquid with a slotted spoon and place on a sheet pan. Use the back of the spoon to half-smash the pieces—you don't want them totally shredded. Broil briefly to crisp and brown.

Beef (or Chicken) Fajitas

Making the best of a lowly cut of tough beef, the dish of marinated and seared skirt steak we know as fajitas (*arracheras* in Mexico) has been satisfying everyone from nineteenth-century cattle-driving cowboys to modern-day foodies. Who hasn't been intoxicated by the aroma and sound of that sizzling cast-iron comal carried aloft through a restaurant dining room? Popularized in the early seventies and now ubiquitous across the state, the Texas-style fajita platter, festooned with salsa, guacamole, cheese, and sour cream, is one of this state's greatest culinary contributions.

Serves 4

¾ cup olive oil

Juice of 4 limes

1 tablespoon Worcestershire sauce

1 tablespoon soy sauce

1 teaspoon salt

1 teaspoon ground black pepper

½ teaspoon paprika

½ teaspoon ground cumin

2 pounds skirt (or flank) steak (or 2 pounds boneless, skinless chicken thighs)

½ red bell pepper, cut into thin strips

½ white onion, cut into thin strips

Tortillas, for serving

Toppings of your choosing: salsas, guacamole, cilantro, onion, etc.

Whisk together the oil, lime juice, Worcestershire sauce, soy sauce, salt, black pepper, paprika, and cumin in a small bowl and pour into a resealable plastic bag. Add the meat, squeeze out the air, and seal. Marinate the meat in the refrigerator for between 4 and 12 hours.

Heat a large cast-iron skillet until it's blazing hot. Remove the steak from the marinade and place in the pan. Cook the steak until desired doneness is achieved, 3 to 4 minutes per side. (Cook the chicken until an internal temperature of 165°F is reached, 7 to 8 minutes per side.) Remove to a cutting board to rest.

Meanwhile, add the bell pepper and onion to the still-hot pan. Sauté, stirring constantly and scraping up any caramelized bits left over from cooking the meat, until the vegetables have softened but still have some bite. Remove from the heat.

Cut the meat into thin strips and serve with the peppers and onions, along with warm tortillas and your choice of toppings.

Calabacitas con Queso

Should you find yourself blessed with hoards of gourds, here's a delicious way to dispense with them, one that doesn't involve bread or fritters. Economical and versatile, calabacitas ("little squashes") is popular in West and South Texas, where it's often served as a side dish, transformed into a main course with the addition of sautéed pork or chicken, or, in this recipe from Austin favorite Veracruz All Natural, wrapped up in a warm tortilla to make a taco.

Makes 6 tacos

2 tablespoons olive oil, divided

½ cup chopped red onion, divided

1 cup cooked black beans, drained

3 teaspoons kosher salt

1 cup cooked long-grain white rice

2 cups sliced zucchini

2 cups sliced yellow squash

2 tablespoons unsalted butter

1 tablespoon minced garlic

1 teaspoon ground black pepper

1 cup diced tomato

1 cup whole-kernel sweet corn

½ cup chopped red bell pepper

¼ jalapeño chile, stem and seeds removed, thinly sliced

12 ounces (1½ cups) queso fresco

2 bay leaves

6 tortillas of your choice, warmed, for serving

6 slices avocado, for serving

¼ cup fresh cilantro leaves, for serving

In a large pot, heat 1 tablespoon of the oil and ¼ cup of the onion over medium-high heat until the onion is very dark, 7 to 8 minutes. Lower the heat, add the black beans, and season with ½ teaspoon of the salt. Mash the mixture until it starts to become creamy. Add the cooked rice and stir to combine. (In Mexico, this is called *casamiento*, which means "marriage.") Set the mixture aside.

Heat the remaining 1 tablespoon oil in a large skillet over high heat, then add the zucchini, squash, butter, minced garlic, the remaining 2½ teaspoons salt, and the black pepper. Cook for 2 to 3 minutes, until softened.

Add the remaining ¼ cup onion, the tomato, corn, bell pepper, and chile. Cook for about 5 minutes, stirring often, until the mixture gets saucy.

Add the queso fresco and bay leaves. Turn off the heat, cover the pan with a lid, and leave until the queso fresco begins to melt, about 3 minutes.

Spread some of the casamiento on a warm tortilla and add the calabacitas. Top with an avocado slice and a sprinkle of cilantro.

The Difference Between Mexican and Tex-Mex

The question is a seemingly simple matter having to do with two delicious things. But like a dark and mysterious mole poblano, the issue is much more complex.

To distinguish one cuisine from the other, a person must first be able to define each of them, which is no easy task. For starters, Mexico is a large country comprising many distinct regions with many distinct foods, all of which can, of course, be rightfully classified as Mexican. Under that big savory umbrella, for example, you've got your norteña cuisine (cabrito, carne asada), your veracruzana cuisine (pescado a la veracruzana, arroz a la tumbada), and your oaxaqueña cuisine (which springs from a state known as Land of the Seven Moles), to name just a few.

The differences among these styles can be as profound as the difference between, say, the pit-smoked brisket you might find in Austin and the oven-baked carrot-and-onion-smothered brisket that you might be served in Brooklyn. So it's important to not paint with too broad a brush when using the term "Mexican food."

And then, too, there's Texas, which if it were to become its own republic again would be the thirty-ninth largest country in the world. Like that of Mexico, the food of Texas is wide-ranging. For instance, there are the three B's (beef, beans, biscuits) of the West Texas cowboy, the seafoods of the coastal regions, the bacon-dripping-drenched delicacies of East Texas's Southern-style traditions, and the German- and Czech-influenced offerings of Central Texas. Kolaches, anyone?

The importance of Mexico's impact on our state's fare is complicated by the fact that Texas was, not so long ago, part of Mexico, which renders Tex-Mex's origins something akin to an enigma wrapped in a tortilla inside a banana leaf on a bed of Spanish rice—smothered in chili con carne. With a side of beans! Black beans!

So, when and where did Tex-Mex originate anyway? Back in 2003, the Texanist's esteemed colleague Patricia Sharpe, who has been surveying the state's gastronomical landscape for decades, addressed this question in *Texas Monthly* with a brief yet insightful history lesson. "What I like to call classic Tex-Mex was born in Texas in the Mexican restaurants run by first- and second-generation immigrants during the first third of the twentieth century," she wrote. "It peaked in a kind of golden age (the color of melted Velveeta, no doubt) that lasted roughly from World War II to the Vietnam War."

The three things that really "put the Tex in Tex-Mex," according to Pat, were yellow American cheese, chili con carne, and the corn tortilla, particularly the deep-fried corn tortilla that allows for the existence of both the crispy taco and the nacho.

The precise value of this hybrid cuisine has been a topic of hot debate for a long time now. Is it just a lesser form of Mexican food, diluted to appeal to Anglos? Is it a shameful example of cultural appropriation? Is it a delightful specimen of cultural *appreciation*? Or is it, perhaps, just another regional Mexican food, like the norteña, veracruzana, and oaxaqueña varieties?

The English-born Mexican cooking authority Diana Kennedy apparently sparked this debate with her best-selling 1972 debut, *The Cuisines of Mexico*, a book credited with changing how Americans perceived Mexican cooking. Kennedy held a low opinion of Americanized takes on the cuisine of her adopted home. "Far too many people know Mexican food as a 'mixed plate': a crisp taco filled with ground meat heavily flavored with an all-purpose chili powder; a soggy tamal covered with a sauce that turns up on everything—too sweet and too overpoweringly onioned—a few fried beans and something else that looks and tastes like all the rest," Kennedy wrote.

Burn! In case you missed it, the "mixed plate"—also sometimes known as the "combination plate" or the "No. 1 Dinner"—that the grande dame of Mexican cooking dismissed so stridently happens to be nothing

less than the Platonic ideal of classic Tex-Mex, though she cast it in as poor a light as possible and failed to note that chips and salsa, more often than not, come gratis, just as the good Lord intended.

Kennedy also neglected to mention that such spreads, when prepared by a skilled hand, are a perfectly satisfactory choice. In fact, there are plenty of Texans who were raised on this sort of Tex-Mex, who love it so much that they've been known to look askance at "weird" Mexican food that strikes them as an existential threat to their beloved cuisine. "Nopales? No, thanks," they'll say.

But is this debate even debatable anymore? In the half century since Kennedy wrote her book and in the nearly two decades since Pat wrote her article, Texas has changed a lot. The state is on the verge of having a Hispanic plurality, and the foods that Texans consume have evolved right alongside our demographics.

There are more ingredients common to Mexico's interior, and more innovation. Tex-Mex barbecue is on the rise. Birria is having a moment, and even Cal-Mex has made inroads. Adding to the fusion confusion—in a delicious way—Asian tacos are now a thing. And Tex-Mex itself is changing too; these days, if one asks for Tex-Mex, one is as likely to be handed oak-smoked brisket in a house-made tortilla as one is a combo platter saturated with chili con Velveeta.

It's high time everyone stop arguing. The war ended, and everybody won. Texans' love for authentic Tex-Mex hasn't stopped authentic Mexican from becoming popular here, and Texans' enthusiasm for authentic Mexican hasn't displaced authentic Tex-Mex. It turns out that in an ever-evolving state like Texas, there's plenty of room for Mexican foods of all tasty stripes. The Texanist advises that you try a little of everything and then eat more of the stuff you like.

¡Buen provecho!

Corn Tortillas

The recipe for corn tortillas is so simple it's a mystery why folks settle for dry, chemical-tasting commodity tortillas that have sat on a grocery store shelf for days. Of course, when you make your own, it can be tough to find that fine line between delicate and sturdy. It requires a little practice. But just about everyone can agree that no taco will ever taste as good on anything but a made-from-scratch corn tortilla.

Makes about 1 dozen tortillas

2 cups masa harina

½ teaspoon salt

1¼ to 1½ cups warm water

Whisk together the masa harina and salt. Add 1 cup of the warm water, stir to combine, and then add a splash of water at a time until you achieve a dough that is smooth and does not crack but is also not sticky.

Divide the dough into about 12 golf ball–size pieces. One at a time, place the dough balls between two pieces of plastic wrap (or a resealable plastic bag that has been cut into two halves), and place on a tortilla press. In one smooth motion, press the ball into a disc and transfer to a skillet over medium-high heat.

Cook each tortilla for about 2 minutes, flipping a few times in the process.

Note: You can roll the dough out with a rolling pin, but tortilla presses are fairly inexpensive and worth owning, especially if you like to make tortillas with any frequency.

Flour Tortillas

Corn tortillas have been with us since the heyday of the Maya and the Aztecs. The flour version came along later, and nowadays commercial versions of these doughy delights are everywhere. But some are still made the old-fashioned way. There's nothing like a puffy, fluffy flour tortilla straight off the hot comal, whether you plan to stuff it full of goodies or merely eat it all by itself, slathered in butter and dusted with salt.

Makes about 1 dozen tortillas

3 cups all-purpose flour

1 teaspoon salt

1 teaspoon baking powder

½ cup shortening, lard, or butter, softened

Warm water, as needed

In a mixing bowl, whisk together the flour, salt, and baking powder.

Add the fat and about ¼ cup warm water. Stir to combine (or combine in a stand mixer). Add more water, a little at a time, as necessary to achieve a pliable yet not sticky texture, almost like Play-Doh. Knead the dough until smooth, 2 to 3 minutes. Form a ball and let rest, covered, for about 30 minutes.

Divide the dough into about 12 golf ball–size pieces. One at a time, on a floured work surface, use a rolling pin to roll the dough into thin 6-inch circles.

Cook each tortilla in a dry skillet or cast-iron skillet over medium heat for about 2 minutes, flipping a few times in the process.

Salsa Roja

For more than two decades, Hope Rodriguez was a *Texas Monthly* staff member beloved not only for her warmth and perpetual good cheer but also for the fact that, twice a week, she would arrive at the office with an insulated case of plump breakfast tacos and a mason jar of still-warm tomato salsa. The tacos were excellent, but the salsa always inspired pleas for the recipe and offers to purchase it by the gallon. Hope, now retired, learned how to make all the basic Tex-Mex dishes when she was thirteen. "My parents owned a restaurant in Cuero," she says, "and they had to be there from early to late." As soon as she was old enough, she was drafted to cook for her brothers and sisters. She learned well. And now we learn from her.

Makes about 1 cup

2 or 3 jalapeño chiles (depending on desired heat), stems removed

3 medium ripe tomatoes

1 small garlic clove, peeled and mashed

2 teaspoons canola oil

½ cup finely chopped white onion

Salt

Roast the chiles on a griddle or in a heavy skillet over medium heat until blistered on all sides, 3 to 4 minutes each side. Remove the chiles and roast the tomatoes in the same pan until cooked and blistered, 15 to 20 minutes.

In a blender, pulse the chiles, tomatoes, and garlic; do not over-puree. Set aside.

In a medium skillet, heat the oil over medium heat, add the onion, and sauté for 3 minutes, until translucent; add the pureed tomato mixture and simmer for about 10 minutes. Season with salt.

Salsa Macha

Within the past five years, this fiery salsa has grown from an obscure garnish to an in-demand item at Texas taquerias and restaurants. In fact, the *New York Times* dubbed it "the most valuable condiment of 2020." Like an Asian chile crisp, the Veracruz-born concoction combines oil, dried chiles, seeds, and nuts into a rusty-red, pastelike sauce that elevates everything it touches. In North Austin, Margarito Pérez makes this batch of salsa macha weekly for his taco truck, Paprika ATX. It's been a customer favorite ever since he opened.

Makes 1 quart

3 cups olive oil

40 garlic cloves, peeled (from 4 to 5 heads)

6 guajillo chiles, stems removed

2 cascabel chiles, stems removed

20 árbol chiles, stems removed

1 ancho chile, stem removed

¾ cup unsalted roasted peanuts

1 tablespoon sesame seeds

¼ cup distilled white vinegar

1 teaspoon salt

In a large, heavy-bottomed pot, heat the oil over medium heat for about 2 minutes. Add the garlic and cook for 1 minute, stirring frequently. Add the chiles and peanuts and cook, stirring, for 2 to 3 more minutes, until the oil starts to turn red but before the garlic begins to burn. Add the sesame seeds, stir, and cook for another 30 seconds. Remove from the heat and let cool for 10 minutes.

Add the mixture to a blender along with the vinegar and salt. Pulse until the mixture has broken down into a pourable consistency but is not completely smooth.

Tomatillo Salsa

Tangy tomatillos play a starring role in this simple green sauce from Valentina's Tex Mex BBQ, in Austin. The addition of spicy habaneros makes for a searing salsa that's a perfect foil for their smoky Brisket Empanadas (page 52), a plate of Migas (page 215), or whatever taco you please.

Makes 3 cups salsa

1 (28-ounce) can tomatillos, drained (see Note)

1 cup fresh cilantro leaves

2 to 3 habanero chiles (depending on your heat preference), stemmed

½ cup diced yellow onion

2 tablespoons fresh lime juice, plus more as needed

1 tablespoon kosher salt, plus more as needed

2 garlic cloves, peeled

Put all the ingredients in a blender and blend until smooth and silky. Taste and add more salt or lime juice if needed.

Note: If you like, you can replace the canned tomatillos with fresh. Boil the tomatillos until soft, remove their skins, and blend them; you'll need about 3½ cups (about 1½ pounds) of blended tomatillo for this recipe.

Salsa Verde

Don't be fooled by this simple three-ingredient salsa: it's so much more than the sum of its parts. It's the signature salsa from Hugo Garcia, of Con Huevos, in San Antonio, who says it "goes great on everything." Lace it into fluffy eggs for breakfast tacos, drizzle it atop crispy chicken flautas, or serve it alongside fat quesadillas stuffed with Oaxaca cheese.

Makes about 2 cups

10 jalapeño chiles, stems removed
3 garlic cloves, peeled
1½ teaspoons salt

In a pot filled with 1 quart water, boil the chiles until darkened, 3 to 4 minutes.

Use a slotted spoon or tongs to remove the chiles from the water and put them into a blender. Add the garlic and salt along with about 2 cups of the water you used to boil the chiles. (Use more water for a thinner salsa, less for a thicker salsa.)

Blend until the garlic is broken down and the salsa has reached the preferred texture. Allow to cool before serving.

Queso

Likely a descendant of queso flameado, the "flamed cheese" of northern Mexico, chili con queso might as well be its own food group in this state. The ridiculously gratifying Tex-Mex fondue is a fixture on restaurant menus and an honored guest at any gathering. But home cooks trying to make something other than the Velveeta standby are often confounded by the whole affair, their hard work resulting in either an oil slick or something akin to igneous rock. The fact is, like it or not, the creamy queso most of us know and love is made with processed cheese. We hope that doesn't offend your epicurean sensibilities.

Makes 1 big bowl of queso

2 tablespoons vegetable oil

½ white onion, diced

1 poblano chile, stem and seeds removed, finely diced

1 jalapeño chile, stem and seeds removed, minced

3 garlic cloves, minced

1 (1-pound) brick processed cheese, such as Velveeta, cut into cubes

1 (10-ounce) can tomatoes and chiles, such as Ro-Tel

1 cup shredded cheddar or Colby cheese

Chopped fresh cilantro and hot sauce, for garnish

In a large heavy-bottomed pot, heat the oil over medium heat. Add the onion, poblano chile, and jalapeño chile; stir until softened, about 4 minutes. Add the garlic and cook for 1 minute more.

A handful at a time, add the processed cheese and stir, allowing each addition to melt before adding the next. Add the tomatoes and chiles and stir to combine. Finally, add the shredded cheese and stir until melted.

Serve immediately in a large bowl topped with cilantro and hot sauce. Alternatively, the queso can be held in a slow cooker set to Warm.

Guacamole

Every year we Texans eat our collective weight in guacamole, which must surely be the avocado's highest calling. Great-tasting "alligator pears" require little more than a sprinkle of salt, but doctoring them up—diced tomatoes, minced garlic, a handful of cilantro, a sprinkle of cumin—is part of the fun. Folks will argue over what does and doesn't belong in a proper guacamole, but you should feel free to just start with a basic recipe, like the one below, and then add whatever appeals to you.

Makes about 2 cups

3 ripe avocados (preferably Hass)

½ small white onion, finely diced

1 jalapeño chile, stem and seeds removed, diced (can use more or less depending on your tolerance for heat)

Lime juice (go easy so as not to overwhelm the avocado)

Salt

In a medium bowl, mash the avocados with a fork, leaving them a little chunky. Add the remaining ingredients, tasting and seasoning with lime juice and salt as you go.

Bean Dip

Fritos Brand Jalapeño Bean Dip, a Fancy Feast–style can of salty *refritos* spiked with fermented chiles, was introduced in 1956 by the San Antonio–born Frito Company, whose salty corn chip had already become a must-have snack all over the country. The dip was enthusiastically marketed to adventure-starved taste buds, a party in a can to take on the road ("Goes Great Outdoors!") or employ at home for "dangerously exciting hors d'oeuvres." And though the original needs no improvement, it's fun to try to replicate it. How hard can it bean?

Makes 1 pint

1 (16-ounce) can refried beans

6 to 8 pickled jalapeño nacho slices, to taste

1 tablespoon brine from the jarred jalapeños

½ teaspoon salt

½ teaspoon sugar

½ teaspoon onion powder

½ teaspoon garlic powder

¼ teaspoon paprika

¼ teaspoon chili powder

¼ teaspoon ground cumin

Dump everything into a food processor and whir it up till smooth. Serve with Fritos.

Composed Nachos

Tortillas go back at least to the Maya and the Aztecs, but it took the Mexican food entrepreneurs of the twentieth century and their deep-fat fryers to fully exploit the tortilla's possibilities. The crispy taco emerged from this felicitous union, but the two most important, and most Texan, variations on the tortilla were the tortilla chip and, in turn, its apotheosis, the nacho. But don't mistake these nachos for the happy-hour platter groaning under the weight of layers of chips, cheese, guacamole, and sour cream. Those are delicious, too, but composed nachos are perfect in their simplicity, each crunchy chip getting an equal share of savory beans, melty cheese, and piquant jalapeño.

Makes 1 large platter of nachos

2 cups vegetable oil, for frying

8 corn tortillas, cut into quarters

Salt

1 (16-ounce) can refried beans

2 cups shredded cheddar or Colby cheese

1 (12-ounce) jar sliced pickled jalapeños (or make your own, page 30)

Optional garnishes: guacamole, cilantro leaves

Preheat the oven to 350°F.

Pour the oil into a large, heavy skillet and heat over medium-high heat (the oil is the right temperature when a piece of tortilla dipped into it bubbles around the edges). Working in batches, fry the tortilla quarters until crispy and golden, 2 to 3 minutes. Using a slotted spoon, remove the chips to a paper towel–lined tray and sprinkle with salt.

Construct the nachos: Place the chips on a sheet pan. Put 1 tablespoon of refried beans on each chip and cover with a large pinch of shredded cheese. Top with 1 slice of pickled jalapeño.

Bake in the oven until the cheese is melted, about 10 minutes. Top with a dab of guacamole and a cilantro leaf or two, if desired.

CHAPTER 4

Home
Plates

BY DAVID COURTNEY

Kitchen-Table Suppers and Backyard Cookouts

Texans are a congenial lot, ready to socialize at the drop of a hat. Heck, the hat really need not even hit the ground; a slight bobble is often all it takes for a gathering to ensue. And whether a particular get-together happens to have been formed for the purpose of marking a birthday, anniversary, retirement, wedding, big game, holiday, or just a Sunday afternoon or a Wednesday night, one thing is certain: there will be vittles.

It's a proven fact that the same way there's usually fire where there's smoke, so are there almost always Texans wherever there's cook fire. And sometimes the impetus for such assemblages is nothing more than that simple and familiar siren song of "Hey, we're grillin' tonight! Y'all wanna come over?" But sizzling steaks (or, perhaps, seared shiitakes for the meat averse) aren't the only draw. No, sir, not by a long shot. The cornucopia of comestibles we're talking about here is as bountiful as it is big, so another guarantee: expect the communal table to be always chock-full of a wide range of delicious offerings.

Sometimes, it's a great big pot of spicy, piping-hot crawfish and new potatoes and cob corn dumped onto a newspaper-covered backyard picnic table. Other times, it is a hot grill full of thick-cut peppery rib eyes or bacon-wrapped fillets or bacon-wrapped dove or bacon-wrapped shrimp spiced up with a sliver of fresh jalapeño, or, yes, cream cheese–stuffed jalapeños that have been caringly—drumroll, please—wrapped in bacon before being thrown on. Maybe it's chicken quarters on the grill. Or it's a venison feast. Redfish or speckled trout might be on the menu, the result of a fruitful fishing excursion on the coast. Perhaps it's those meaty shiitakes! Or just an enormous medley of vegetables like onion, bell pepper, carrot, squash, zucchini, and asparagus. The best asparagus, as everyone knows, is char-grilled asparagus. It could also be an unofficial backyard chili cookoff with otherwise friendly neighbors going head-to-head for bragging rights to the best bowl of red. Sometimes, there's ice-cold beer or chilled wine or fresh-made margaritas. Usually all three.

Other times, the festivities might be just a smidge less, well, festive, which isn't necessarily a bad thing. We can't go full bore all the time, after all. Maybe the standard post–Sunday service trip to the local Luby's has been scrapped in lieu of a trip to Aunt Nino's (full disclosure: I had an actual Aunt Nino while growing up in Central Texas and this sort of detour was not unusual) for one of her whole-afternoon-and-into-the-evening-long lunches. Maybe she'll make her crisp-to-perfection fried chicken. If so, there's sure to be buttery mashed potatoes, and lemony steamed broccoli, and baskets of yeast rolls. Or perhaps she'll serve up chicken-fried steak. Or golden fried catfish and homemade hush puppies. Enchiladas! And Spanish rice and ranch beans and piping-hot tortillas. And homemade jalapeño cornbread! Or it's a comforting King Ranch casserole. Maybe there'll be that weird tomato aspic for a starter. "Hell, I hope not," I prayed in church as a young man, determined to never even sample a tomato aspic. There's no question about dessert, though. The kitchen counter will be a sea of them: homemade apple pie and pecan pie and rich brownies and even richer chocolate sheet cake. Oh, thank you, Lord!

Whether one happens to be a generous host or a lucky attendee, gathering with friends and family for a little fellowship—especially when there's a spread of mouthwatering victuals within reach—is what makes the world go 'round. Or at least makes it worth living on while it goes around.

King Ranch Casserole

A staple of school lunchrooms and church suppers, frat houses and funerals, the King Ranch casserole does not, as far as anyone can tell, hail from the legendary King Ranch. More likely it's a Junior League attempt at chilaquiles or a Texas take on chicken à la king. And though it is a member in good standing of the condensed-soup canon, those bland, oddly comforting turkey tetrazzinis and tuna noodles simply cannot compete with the King Ranch, whose lively Tex-Mex flavors— spicy chili powder, zesty roasted peppers, earthy mushrooms—coalesce in one sublime, admittedly unattractive package. Ditch the cans (except for the wholly respectable Ro-Tel) and make this from-scratch version.

Makes one 9 x 13-inch pan

For the chicken

1 (4-pound) whole chicken (or equivalent in bone-in, skin-on pieces)

1 white onion, peeled and cut in half

6 garlic cloves, peeled and smashed

1 jalapeño chile, stem removed, cut in half

1 bay leaf

1 teaspoon black peppercorns

1 teaspoon cumin seeds

1 tablespoon salt

For the sauce

½ cup (1 stick) unsalted butter

1 white onion, diced

4 garlic cloves, minced

1 red bell pepper, diced

1 celery stalk, finely diced

1 jalapeño chile, stem and seeds removed, minced

Salt and ground black pepper

1 (8-ounce) package white mushrooms, finely diced

½ cup all-purpose flour

1 teaspoon ground cumin

1 teaspoon chili powder

½ teaspoon dried oregano

1 teaspoon hot sauce (dealer's choice)

TO MAKE THE CHICKEN:

Add the chicken, onion, garlic, chile, bay leaf, peppercorns, cumin seeds, and salt to a large, heavy-bottomed pot; cover the chicken with water. Bring to a boil, reduce the heat to maintain a simmer, and simmer uncovered until the chicken is cooked through, about 1 hour. (Skim the surface of the water as needed to keep the stock clear.)

Remove the chicken from the pot and set aside to cool. When the chicken is cool enough to handle, pull the meat into bite-size pieces. Discard the skin and bones.

Strain the stock into another pot and continue simmering to reduce until the stock is needed, about 30 minutes. You should have about 4 cups of stock in all; if you have more than that, you can freeze the rest for another use.

TO MAKE THE SAUCE:

In a deep, wide skillet or Dutch oven, melt the butter over medium heat, then add the onion, garlic, bell pepper, celery, and chile, along with a healthy amount of salt and pepper. Sauté, stirring, until the vegetables have softened, about 3 minutes. Add the mushrooms and sauté for 8 minutes more, or until the vegetables have released most of their liquid and you can once again see melted butter in the bottom of the pan.

(cont.)

1 (10-ounce) can tomatoes with chiles, such as Ro-Tel

1 cup heavy cream

For the casserole

12 corn tortillas

2 cups shredded cheese, such as mild cheddar or Colby jack

Sprinkle with the flour and stir for a minute or two, to take the raw edge off the flour. Stir in the cumin, chili powder, oregano, and hot sauce. Add 4 cups of the reserved chicken stock, stir to combine, and let come to a simmer. Simmer until thickened; the sauce should be gravy-like. Add the canned tomatoes with chiles, stir to combine, then add the cream and stir again. Add the shredded chicken and adjust the seasoning.

TO ASSEMBLE AND BAKE THE CASSEROLE:

Preheat the oven to 350°F. Grease a 9 x 13-inch baking pan.

Add a cup or so of the sauce to the bottom of the prepared pan. Cover with a layer of tortilla, a layer of sauce, and a layer of cheese; repeat until you run out of ingredients, ending with a layer of cheese. Bake until bubbling and browned, about 1 hour.

Caribbean-Style Shrimp and Slow Cooker Grits

When it comes to Gulf shrimp, chef Nicola Blaque, of the Jerk Shack, in San Antonio, likes to slather them in a spicy Caribbean marinade, sauté them in olive oil, and serve them over decadent grits that have been hanging out in a slow cooker all day. This recipe couldn't be easier, or more satisfying. As a bonus, it also feeds a crowd.

Serves 6

For the grits

Nonstick cooking spray

1½ cups stone-ground grits

6 cups water

2 teaspoons salt

1½ cups buttermilk

½ cup (1 stick) unsalted butter

Salt and ground black pepper

For the shrimp marinade

1 bunch fresh flat-leaf parsley, roughly chopped

1 bunch fresh thyme, stems removed

1 bunch green onions, roughly chopped

6 garlic cloves, peeled

Zest and juice from 1 lemon

2 habanero chiles, stems removed

2 tablespoons onion powder

2 tablespoons brown sugar

3 tablespoons salt

2 tablespoons garlic powder

3 teaspoons coarsely ground black pepper

1 teaspoon ground allspice

1 teaspoon smoked paprika

½ teaspoon ground cinnamon

½ teaspoon ground nutmeg

½ teaspoon ground cloves

TO MAKE THE GRITS:

Spray the crock of a slow cooker with cooking spray. Add the grits, water, and salt. Cover and cook on low for at least 7 hours or overnight.

Before serving, add the buttermilk and butter and season with salt and pepper.

TO MAKE THE MARINADE:

Combine all the ingredients in a blender and blend until smooth.

(cont.)

¼ teaspoon ground cumin

¼ cup soy sauce

¼ cup olive oil

2 tablespoons water

For the shrimp

2 pounds large Texas Gulf shrimp, peeled and deveined

¼ cup shrimp marinade

3 tablespoons olive oil

4 tablespoons (½ stick) unsalted butter

Juice of 1 lemon

Sliced green onions, for serving

TO MAKE THE SHRIMP:

Place the shrimp in a resealable plastic bag and cover with the marinade. (Reserve any unused marinade for another use. See Note.) Refrigerate for 1 hour.

Heat a large skillet over medium-high heat. Add the oil and shrimp. Do not overcrowd the skillet, because you want it to remain hot. You can cook in two batches if needed. Once the shrimp are cooked, add the butter and lemon juice and stir until the butter is melted.

Ladle the slow-cooked grits into a bowl, top with the shrimp, and sprinkle with green onions.

Note: Leftover marinade may be kept in an airtight container in the refrigerator for up to a week and is delicious with chicken or pork.

Braised Chicken and Black Pepper Dumplings

Chris Shepherd—perhaps Houston's most famous chef, James Beard Award winner, and tireless champion of the city's immigrant-driven culinary scene—elevates this Southern staple as only he can. A creamy chicken base cradles peppery, fluffy dumplings for a dish that's as luxurious as it is comforting.

Serves 6

For the chicken

2 bay leaves

3 garlic cloves, peeled

2 celery stalks, chopped

1 large yellow onion, chopped

1 (3-pound) chicken (or 3 pounds of bone-in, skin-on pieces)

¼ cup heavy cream

1 tablespoon Louisiana hot sauce

1½ tablespoons Worcestershire sauce

Salt and ground black pepper

For the dumplings

1 cup all-purpose flour

½ teaspoon sugar

1½ teaspoons baking powder

½ teaspoon salt

2 teaspoons ground black pepper

4 tablespoons cold unsalted butter, cubed

⅓ cup buttermilk

Sliced green onion and chopped dill, for garnish

TO MAKE THE CHICKEN:

Place the bay leaves, garlic, celery, onion, and chicken in a large stockpot and cover with water. Bring to a boil, then lower the heat to maintain a simmer and cook for 1½ hours, skimming any foam that rises to the surface. Carefully pull the chicken out of the pot and set aside to cool slightly.

Once the chicken is cool enough to handle, pull the meat into bite-size shreds and set aside. Discard the skin and bones.

Strain the stock into another stockpot. If there's a lot of fat on the surface, you can skim some off. Bring to a simmer. Add the cream, hot sauce, and Worcestershire sauce and simmer for 20 minutes. Season with salt and pepper.

TO MAKE THE DUMPLINGS AND SERVE:

Combine the flour, sugar, baking powder, salt, and black pepper in a large bowl, then add the butter and stir to combine. Add the buttermilk and mix by hand until just combined.

While the soup is simmering, use a large spoon to slowly drop spoonfuls of the dumpling mixture into the soup. Poach the dumplings until cooked through, about 6 minutes.

Add the pulled chicken back into the soup and season with salt and pepper. Ladle into soup bowls and garnish with sliced green onion and dill.

Green Chile Hominy

The James Beard Award–winning Perini Ranch Steakhouse, in tiny Buffalo Gap, is a destination restaurant serving up elevated Texas comfort food alongside loads of Texas hospitality. This is one of the restaurant's simpler recipes, but it's as decadent as it gets.

Serves 8

10 slices bacon

1 cup chopped white onion

2 (4-ounce) cans chopped green chiles, drained (about 1 cup)

4 (15-ounce) cans white hominy, drained, with ½ cup of the liquid reserved

1 tablespoon pickled jalapeño brine

½ pound cheddar cheese, grated

Preheat the oven to 325°F.

In a large, deep skillet or Dutch oven, fry the bacon over medium heat until crisp, about 6 minutes. Remove the bacon from the pan and chop it. Pour off all but about 2 tablespoons of the fat. Add the onions to the remaining bacon fat in the pan and cook until transparent, about 4 minutes.

Add three-quarters of the bacon and three-quarters of the chiles to the onions, along with the hominy. Add the reserved hominy liquid and pickled jalapeño brine, stir to combine, and bring to a boil.

One handful at a time, stir in three-quarters of the cheese until melted.

Pour the hominy mixture into a 9 x 13-inch baking dish.

Combine the last quarter of the bacon, the chiles, and cheese, and sprinkle over the hominy.

Bake until the cheese on top is melted, about 15 minutes. Serve as a hearty side dish to a meaty main course.

Tex-Mex Cornbread

Chili and cornbread. Beans and cornbread. Stuffing with cornbread. The crumbly round of salty-sweet cornmeal is included in the cast of many menus, but it often gets stuck in a supporting role. This adaptation enlivens the classic recipe with a zesty zip of green chiles, a festive pop of fresh corn, and the salty tang of cheddar cheese. Crowned with a pat of butter and flanked by a cold beer, there's no reason cornbread can't be the lone star of a satisfying Texas meal.

Makes one 8-inch round cornbread

2 tablespoons bacon drippings or vegetable oil

1 cup coarse stone-ground yellow cornmeal

¼ cup all-purpose flour

1½ teaspoons baking powder

1 teaspoon kosher salt

1 egg

1 cup buttermilk

¼ cup corn kernels, cut from the cob or frozen

¼ cup diced sweet onion

¼ cup chopped poblano chiles (or any type of green chile)

½ cup shredded cheddar or longhorn cheese

Grease an 8-inch cast-iron skillet with the bacon drippings, then place in the oven and heat to 450°F.

Mix the cornmeal, flour, baking powder, and salt in a medium bowl. Whisk the egg with the buttermilk, then add to the bowl of dry ingredients. Add the corn, onion, chiles, and cheese and stir until just combined.

Remove the skillet from the oven and pour the melted drippings into the batter (there won't be much). Give the batter a quick stir, then pour it into the skillet. Bake for 20 minutes, or until the top is golden brown and a toothpick inserted into the center comes out clean. Cut into wedges and serve.

Chawanmushi

This savory steamed egg custard is often served as an appetizer in Japanese restaurants, and Austin-based izakaya Kemuri Tatsu-Ya offers it chilled and decorated with seasonal garnishes. But it's also beloved by home cooks, especially since it makes for a great way to use up leftovers. The restaurant recommends adding poached chicken, shiitake mushrooms, or toasted ginkgo nuts (see Note), but consider this dish a canvas for your imagination.

Serves 4 as a side or appetizer

For the dashi

1 small sheet dried kombu, about 2-by-4 inches

1 cup filtered water

2 tablespoons bonito flakes

For the chawanmushi

1 extra-large egg, preferably pasture-raised

¾ cup dashi

2 tablespoons mirin

½ teaspoon good-quality soy sauce

Pinch salt

Chopped Japanese parsley (mitsuba) or scallions, to garnish

TO MAKE THE DASHI:

Soak the kombu in a bowl with the filtered water overnight. The next day, bring the kombu and water to a light simmer over high heat—be careful not to let it boil. Turn off the heat and add the bonito flakes. Resist the urge to stir, as this will cloud the broth. Let steep, undisturbed, for 5 minutes. Strain the dashi through a cheesecloth and chill.

TO MAKE THE CHAWANMUSHI:

Use a fork to gently whisk the egg in a small bowl, taking care to not incorporate any air. Add the dashi, mirin, soy sauce, and salt to the egg and gently stir to combine. Pour through a mesh strainer into a measuring cup with a pour spout.

Divide the mixture evenly among 4 shallow, heatproof vessels with lids. We recommend chawanmushi cups, canning jars, or ramekins covered with foil.

Carefully place the cups into a bamboo (or other style) steamer and steam for about 10 minutes, until just set.

Garnish the custards with parsley or scallions and serve immediately, or chill and serve cold.

Note: Before steaming, you may add poached chicken thighs, scored shiitake caps, or toasted ginkgo nuts to the custard mixture. If you prefer larger portions, you may increase the portion to 4 ounces per person (for three servings) and increase the steaming time to 15 minutes.

The Texanist is *Texas Monthly* senior editor David Courtney.

THE TEXANIST ON

The Origins of the Texas Sheet Cake

When it comes to sheet cakes, the Texanist is a shameless homer. The simple, sweet, chocolaty goodness that is the Texas version outshines all the other states' sheet cakes by a country mile. Have you ever had the displeasure of choking down a slice of Michigan sheet cake? Neither has the Texanist, but the mere thought of it is making the hair on the back of his neck stand up. Known by such alternative monikers as Texas brownie cake, Texas ranch cake, Texas sheath cake (the Texanist owes his dear old mother-in-law an apology for the years of loudly mocking what he always thought was her mispronunciation of *sheet*), and, simply, Texas cake, this confection has been a favorite for cake-worthy occasions in the Lone Star State (and elsewhere) for a long time. Cake authorities have yet to pinpoint its exact origin, but they have determined that it was not a personal recipe of Lady Bird Johnson's, as many believe it to be, and that the name is probably owed to either the cake's large size or its oily richness. The Texanist would urge you to try to make one yourself. And go ahead and save him a slice.

Texas Sheet Cake

Texans have a proprietary interest in this enormous rectangle of thin, flat chocolate cake slathered in deliciously sugary, pecan-studded chocolate icing. What exactly makes it a "Texas" sheet cake? Some maintain it's because it's flamboyantly rich. Others point to the addition of Texas-y ingredients like buttermilk and pecans. Still others say it's simply because the cake is huge. Everything is bigger in Texas, after all.

Makes one 10 x 15-inch cake (about 24 slices)

For the cake

½ cup (1 stick) unsalted butter, plus more for the pan

2 cups all-purpose flour, plus more for the pan

½ cup buttermilk

2 large eggs

1 teaspoon vanilla extract

1 teaspoon baking soda

2 cups sugar

1 teaspoon ground cinnamon

½ teaspoon salt

½ cup vegetable shortening

6 tablespoons cocoa powder

1 cup water

For the icing

½ cup (1 stick) unsalted butter

6 tablespoons buttermilk

6 tablespoons cocoa powder

1 teaspoon vanilla extract

1 pound powdered sugar

1 cup pecan pieces, plus more for sprinkling on top

TO MAKE THE CAKE:

Preheat the oven to 400°F. Butter and flour a half-sheet cake pan (10 x 15 inches).

In a large bowl, combine the buttermilk, eggs, vanilla, and baking soda. Whisk until smooth and set aside.

In another large bowl, sift the flour, sugar, cinnamon, and salt. Set aside.

In a medium saucepan, combine the butter, shortening, cocoa, and water and bring to a boil over high heat.

Pour the hot mixture over the flour and stir vigorously with a wooden spoon. Add the buttermilk mixture and stir until combined.

Pour the batter into the prepared pan and bake for 20 minutes, or until the edges of the cake pull away from the pan and the cake springs back when you touch it.

TO MAKE THE ICING:

About 10 minutes before the cake is done, combine the butter, buttermilk, and cocoa in a large pot and bring to a boil. Quickly remove from the heat (it will not be pretty) and add the vanilla and powdered sugar. Beat with an electric mixer until smooth. Stir in the pecan pieces.

Spread the icing over the hot cake. If desired, sprinkle more pecan pieces on top. Let cool, then cut into squares and serve.

Grilled Rib Eye

When it comes to the art of selecting and cooking a good steak, it seems as if you need an advanced degree from A&M in order to confidently ruminate on such complexities as marbling scores, grass-fed beef versus grain-fed, and dry aging versus wet. Your best bet? Consult your butcher, bring home the nicest piece of meat your wallet will allow, and introduce it to a little salt and pepper and an open flame. The merits of such an uncomplicated approach were readily apparent to no less a bovine authority than Texas man of letters J. Frank Dobie, of whose technique his buddy and fellow writer Walter Prescott Webb said, "He wants a green stick with the steak speared on it.... If he can drop it a time or two in the ashes, he considers the flavor improved."

Serves 1 to 2

1 well-marbled rib eye, at least 1 inch thick

2 tablespoons olive oil

Salt and ground black pepper

Take the steak out of the refrigerator 30 minutes before cooking. Rub the steak with the oil, then generously dust with salt and pepper.

Get the grill going, with the charcoal or wood off to one side. Once the coals are established, sear the steak on both sides directly over the heat (you want a nice set of grill marks), then move it to the side of the grill that's not directly above the coals. Close the lid.

Cook until the steak has reached the desired temperature on an instant-read thermometer (between 130 and 135°F for medium-rare). Flip the steak a few times while it cooks, and keep in mind that thicker steaks will take longer.

Remove the steak from the grill and let it rest for at least 5 minutes. Cut into slices against the grain and serve.

ODE TO THE
Rib Eye

Cutting into a deftly seared, pepper-crusted rib eye to reveal its ruby interior brings a quiver to your hand, perhaps a catch in your throat: You want the moment to last, but you can't endure the suspense. There's nothing like that first bite, that tandem brush of satiny meat and caramelized edge against your lips. It's enough to make you close your eyes and give thanks that you're in Texas, where rib eye rules as the king of steaks. It only goes to reason that Texans hold this steak in higher regard than most other folks, for ours is the largest beef-producing state in the nation. And though it was once the T-bone that was celebrated, today's heirs of the legendary cattle range know that a rib eye's abundant marbling and depth of flavor trump all others. So take that bite. Fat be damned. —*June Naylor*

Seekh Kebabs

The Texas tradition of fire-kissed beef meets Indian spices in these skewers, a contribution from *Texas Monthly* reader and home cook Ranganath "Ron" Habbu, of Colleyville, who says he likes to serve them warm with thin-sliced red onion, a lime wedge, and mint leaves. They taste even better, he says, during a game: "Helps soften the blow of typical Cowboys meltdowns on Sundays. Sigh."

Serves 3 to 4

½ yellow onion, finely diced

1-inch piece ginger, peeled and finely diced

½ cup finely chopped fresh cilantro

1 jalapeño or serrano chile (depending on desired heat level), stem removed, finely chopped

1 teaspoon salt

¼ teaspoon baking soda

1 pound ground beef (80/20)

Soak the wooden skewers in water for 10 to 30 minutes.

Combine all the ingredients except the beef and stir to combine.

Add the beef and mix thoroughly. (Note: If you think you're done mixing, keep going a bit longer.)

Shape into fat sausages around wooden skewers and grill over high heat until cooked through and browned, about 5 minutes per side.

Lao Beef Skewers

This dish is a customer favorite at Bob Somsith's Austin food truck SXSE Food Co., even though beef is not heavily consumed back in his homeland of Laos. "But in the US—and especially in Texas—beef is what's for dinner," he says. "For the most part, we use cheaper cuts of meat to prepare our meals, and rib eye is not the first choice of most Laotians in America. Rib eye is reserved for special occasions and for welcoming guests from afar. The younger generation is changing that, however. And at SXSE, it's our signature dish."

Serves 4 to 6

For the basting sauce

½ cup oyster sauce

¾ cup hoisin sauce

2 tablespoons fish sauce

1 tablespoon sriracha

¼ cup water

1 tablespoon garlic powder

1 teaspoon kosher salt

½ teaspoon ground black pepper

1 tablespoon sugar

2 teaspoons ground dried lemongrass

For the jeow som (dipping sauce)

6 garlic cloves, finely minced

1 red Thai chile, finely chopped

1-inch piece fresh ginger, peeled and finely chopped

½ teaspoon kosher salt

2 teaspoons sugar

⅓ cup fish sauce (Somsith prefers Three Crabs brand)

⅓ cup fresh lime juice

For the beef skewers

2 pounds rib eye, cut into 1½-inch cubes and pierced with bamboo skewers (soak in water for 10 to 30 minutes before using), with 4 cubes per skewer

Basting sauce

Jeow som

Cooked jasmine or sticky rice, for serving

TO MAKE THE BASTING SAUCE:

Add all the ingredients to a bowl and whisk vigorously to combine.

TO MAKE THE JEOW SOM:

In the bowl of a food processor, combine the garlic, chile, ginger, salt, and sugar. Process until a paste forms. Add the fish sauce and lime juice and pulse to combine.

TO MAKE THE BEEF SKEWERS:

Heat a grill until it's very hot.

Use a brush to baste each skewer up and down and on all sides until evenly coated with the basting sauce. Cook, turning frequently, about 12 minutes total for medium-rare, until the beef reaches the desired char or internal temperature. Serve with rice and jeow som, for dipping.

Grilled Jalapeño Poppers

The very definition of a crowd-pleaser, the grilled jalapeño popper is a less-involved affair than its deep-fried cousin (page 188). Instead, grilled poppers are simply halved jalapeños spread with cream cheese and wrapped in bacon. You can buy them premade at plenty of grocery stores across Texas, but they're easy enough to make. And if you show up to a party with a trayful, you'll be sure to secure a second invitation.

Makes 2 dozen

1 dozen jalapeño chiles, halved lengthwise, seeds removed

1 (8-ounce) package cream cheese

12 slices bacon, cut in half

Spread about 1 tablespoon of cream cheese onto each jalapeño half. Wrap a slice of bacon crosswise around each half and secure with a toothpick. At this point, the poppers can be refrigerated until ready to grill.

Over a medium-hot grill (about 350°F), cook over indirect heat with the lid closed, until the bacon is rendered and crisp, the chiles are cooked through, and the cream cheese is just beginning to brown, about 30 minutes. (You can also bake them in a 350°F oven for the same amount of time.) Let cool for 5 minutes (if you can wait that long!) and serve.

Suzie's Okra Salad

Okra grows in great abundance in Texas, and though there are those who abhor the somewhat slimy pod, plenty of others enjoy it stewed, pickled, and, of course, fried. That's the form it takes in this salad from *Texas Monthly* staffer Cassandra Fortson, who says the secret to her former neighbor's recipe is using bacon grease in the dressing. "It made me eat okra," Fortson says, "and I was the pickiest child ever!"

Makes 1 party-size bowl of okra salad

¼ cup finely diced red onion

1 green bell pepper, finely diced

¾ cup trimmed and sliced green onions

1 pint cherry tomatoes, halved

1 (12-ounce) package thick-cut bacon, chopped

1 tablespoon red wine vinegar

1 tablespoon distilled white vinegar

¼ cup olive oil

1 (32-ounce) bag frozen breaded okra

Salt and ground black pepper

In a medium bowl, combine the red onion, bell pepper, green onions, and cherry tomatoes. Set aside.

Heat a skillet over medium heat and brown the chopped bacon, about 12 minutes. Remove the bacon bits to a paper towel–lined plate and, once cooled, add to the tomato mixture. Leave the bacon grease in the pan.

In a small bowl, whisk together 1 tablespoon of the bacon grease, the red wine vinegar, distilled white vinegar, and oil to make a dressing. Season with salt and pepper. Pour half the dressing on the tomato-bacon mixture, stir to coat, and refrigerate.

Heat the remaining bacon grease over medium heat. Fry the okra in batches, flipping them after a minute or two so they turn evenly golden. Remove to a paper towel–lined plate.

When all the okra is cooked, fold it into the vegetable and bacon mixture. Drizzle additional dressing over the top and serve at room temperature.

Texas Caviar

Unlike many of the dishes in this book, Texas caviar has a definitive origin story: Helen Corbitt, cookbook author and longtime head chef at Neiman Marcus, invented it in 1940, as part of a meal highlighting Texas ingredients. Admittedly not a fan of the legumes, Corbitt decided to mask their flavor by pickling them with garlic and onions, to great success. Modern riffs add corn, peppers, and cilantro, even tomatoes or black beans. But no matter how you like your Texas caviar, make sure you serve it with tortilla chips.

Serves 8

2 (15.5-ounce) cans black-eyed peas, drained (or 4 cups home-cooked black-eyed peas)

1 jalapeño chile, stem and seeds removed, minced

2 red bell peppers, stems and seeds removed, diced

1 small red onion, diced

1 cup corn kernels, defrosted if frozen

3 tablespoons olive oil

Juice of 2 limes

1 teaspoon salt

¼ teaspoon ground cumin

¼ cup chopped fresh cilantro (optional)

In a large bowl, combine the black-eyed peas, chile, bell peppers, red onion, and corn. Stir to combine.

In a small bowl, whisk together the oil, lime juice, salt, and cumin. Dress the vegetables with the dressing, stirring to coat, and refrigerate for at least 1 hour before serving (it can be made the day before).

Just before serving, add the cilantro, if desired, and stir to combine.

Pasta Salad

Classically, a pasta salad is a clean-out-the-refrigerator affair: a creamy mayonnaise dressing, macaroni, and whatever needs using up. In this version, bacon and pickled jalapeños add enough smoke, sass, and spice to render it quintessentially Texan, but beyond that, you can make this your own. Replace the tomatoes with diced bell pepper, corn kernels, or chopped broccoli—the sky's the limit.

Serves 6

6 slices thick-cut bacon, diced

1 cup mayonnaise

1 teaspoon salt

1 teaspoon ground black pepper

¼ cup diced pickled jalapeños, plus 2 tablespoons pickling brine

1 pound macaroni, cooked according to the directions on the package

1 bunch scallions, chopped

1 cup cherry tomatoes, cut in half

In a large skillet, brown the bacon over medium heat, stirring occasionally. Use a slotted spoon to remove the bacon to a paper towel–lined plate.

In a small bowl, whisk together the mayonnaise, salt, pepper, and pickling brine.

In a large bowl, combine the macaroni, pickled jalapeños, scallions, and cherry tomatoes. Stir to combine, then add the dressing. Stir until coated. Refrigerate for at least 1 hour before serving.

All Hail Helen Corbitt, Who Delivered Us from the Canned Fruit Cocktail

In the years BC (before Corbitt), Texans had no artichokes, no fresh raspberries, no herbs except decorative parsley, only beef (chicken-fried, barbecued, or well-done), potatoes (fried or mashed and topped with a glop of cream gravy), and wedges of iceberg with sweet orange dressing. Fruit salad meant canned pears or pineapple with a dollop of mayonnaise and a grating of cheddar cheese. Canned asparagus was a remarked-upon delicacy, as were Le Sueur canned peas. The introduction of the TV dinner in the fifties would be a step up for some households.

Into this bleak culinary landscape came a young Irish Catholic Yankee named Helen Corbitt. In a career that spanned nearly forty years in Texas, she delivered us from canned fruit cocktail, plates of fried brown food, and too much bourbon and branch into a world of airy soufflés, poached fish, chanterelle mushrooms, fresh salsify, Major Grey's Chutney, crisp steamed vegetables, and fine wine. She was a creative pioneer who came here reluctantly and learned to love us. She taught us, she fed us, she entertained us, and best of all, before she left us in 1978, she wrote down the how-to of Corbitt hospitality in five cookbooks, giving us confidence that the civilizing pleasures of the table were within our reach. Superstar Texas chefs may pay homage to Julia Child and Simone Beck, but long before they learned to clarify butter, there was Corbitt.

Helen Corbitt was born on January 25, 1906, in upstate New York into a home where good food was highly valued and generously shared. After her graduation from Skidmore College, in Saratoga Springs, with a degree in home economics, her plans for medical school were derailed by the Depression. She took a job as a therapeutic dietitian at Presbyterian Hospital in Newark, New Jersey, then went on to Cornell Medical Center in New York, where she persuaded doctors that sick people would respond more favorably to food if it was properly seasoned and attractively served.

In 1940 Corbitt was offered a job teaching catering and restaurant management at the University of Texas. "I said, 'Who the hell wants to go to Texas?'" she later told *Dallas Times Herald* reporter Julia Sweeney. "Only I didn't say 'hell' in those days. I learned to swear in Texas." Two weeks after she arrived in Austin, she was asked to do a dinner for a hotel convention using only Texas products: "What I thought of Texas products wasn't fit to print!" Like an alchemist, she transformed prosaic black-eyed peas for the dinner, adding some garlic, onion, vinegar, and oil and christening them Texas Caviar. Neiman Marcus would later sell thousands of cans of the stuff.

Corbitt left Austin for a more lucrative position at the Houston Country Club in 1942. She still wasn't sold on Texas and planned to stay just long enough to get on her feet and buy a ticket back to New York. She claimed that she didn't unpack her suitcase for the first six months. But after a year in Houston, she had decided to stay. "I was having such a good time producing great food for appreciative Texans," she told her literary agent, Elizabeth Ann Johnson. She miraculously turned out fancy dinners despite World War II rationing. Unable to get Wesson oil, she reportedly bought No. 1 refined mineral oil from the Humble Oil Company and used it for cooking purposes. "The people at the Houston Country Club were awfully healthy while I was there," she told Sweeney.

Joske's Department Store in Houston hired her away from the country club to manage its restaurant and catering, but the job wasn't a good fit. "Being fired from Joske's [for not bringing in enough money and not seeing eye to eye with the executives] was the best thing that ever happened to me," she said. She returned to Austin in the early fifties to reign over the Driskill Hotel's dining room and catering, introducing politicians and other dignitaries to food creatively prepared and properly served. Clarence "Captain" White, whom she trained to oversee the Driskill dining room, remembered, "When we served fresh asparagus, she always had us cut it on the bias, so it would look like green beans. The men would sometimes say, 'What kind of green beans are these? I like 'em!'" Recalled Lady Bird Johnson: "When Lyndon and [longtime friend] Jesse Kellam had dinner parties at the Driskill, they always knew the evening would go well if Helen Corbitt was in charge." According to Bess Abell, the White House social secretary in the Johnson years, Helen Corbitt recipes were frequently used at the White House. Her signature flowerpot dessert was a natural for Mrs. Johnson's beautification luncheons. Years before anybody had heard of Martha Stewart, Corbitt layered tiny clay flowerpots with cake and ice cream, stuck a trimmed drinking straw in the middle, and topped off the pot with meringue. After the meringue was browned in the oven, she inserted a fresh flower in each straw. These desserts frequently pop up at Texas bridesmaids' luncheons even today.

In 1955, after being courted for several years, Corbitt finally agreed to take over Neiman Marcus's food service. It is difficult to say who benefited more from the relationship. Neiman's flagship Dallas store was in its heyday. Texans had money and were spending it. Women still wore hats and gloves downtown, and the

Zodiac Room, where men and women sipped Corbitt's tiny cups of chicken consommé while sleek models sporting the latest fashions circled their tables, was an oasis of sophistication and glamour. Corbitt had the flair, the taste, and the energy to produce food that was as visually enchanting as the store's windows on Main and Commerce. She was a cosmopolitan woman with a thorough knowledge of the best restaurants and food suppliers in the country. But most important, she understood Texans and delighted in getting them to eat foods that they professed to abhor, like lamb, anchovies, and yogurt. The assurance of good taste that Neiman Marcus's customers sought in the store's chic ready-to-wear could now be extended to their dining tables as well. "When Miss Corbitt put white grapes, heavy cream, and slivered toasted almonds in her chicken salad, it gave the rest of us confidence to experiment a bit," said one of her ardent followers.

The experiments didn't always work. Mary Bloom, who worked at Neiman's as a young woman, remembers asking Miss Corbitt to take a look at a dinner party menu she was planning for friends. "I'm trying to be creative the way you are," Mary said. "See, I'm going to peel the cantaloupe and stuff it with Roquefort cheese." Miss Corbitt paused and then, unleashing her famous Irish wit, said, "Mary, am I the first to tell you that you're pregnant?" She was.

Stanley Marcus, in a foreword to a posthumous collection of Corbitt's recipes, wrote of her fourteen-year tenure at the helm of the Zodiac Room: "She was difficult, for she knew the difference between better and best, and she was never willing to settle for second best." He dubbed her his Wild Irish Genius and the Balenciaga of Food. "Too many chefs today regard themselves first as artists," Marcus said. "Corbitt created a beautiful plate, but she gave greater attention to how the food would taste."

Corbitt had what these days we might call healthy self-esteem. She told Julia Sweeney about the time a produce clerk caught her picking out the freshest mushrooms in the back room at the Simon David specialty food store and said, "I'm sorry, but the manager doesn't allow people back here." She blithely responded, "Go tell the manager Helen Corbitt is here. I have pickin' privileges." But Corbitt's perfectionism exacted a price: even though it was packed with people daily, the Zodiac Room never showed a profit. In his memoir *Minding the Store*, Marcus wrote that, when he complained of heavy losses, she replied, "You didn't mention money when you employed me. You simply said that you wanted the best food in the country. I've given you that."

Soups in the Zodiac Room were always made from scratch, with one exception: the cream of tomato. In a 1972 interview with *Dallas Morning News* food writer Francis Raffetto, Corbitt admitted, "I used Campbell's, with coffee cream and butter to make it like velvet." New York playwright Moss Hart, having lunch one day in the late fifties with Marcus's brother Edward, ordered a second bowl and then asked for the recipe. To Marcus's chagrin, Corbitt refused. She later explained, "We couldn't tell Moss Hart he ate Campbell's soup at Neiman Marcus."

Helen Corbitt cooked for the smartly dressed country club set and for movie stars and socialites. She entertained royalty and the dignitaries of many countries, but she also cooked for the secretaries and shopgirls and housewives who sometimes treated themselves to a pastry or a sandwich at the standup counter on the main floor. "Each bite of those little sandwiches was like a gift," one woman recalled. "They were generously spread, and there was always something surprising in a Helen Corbitt sandwich—a little pineapple in the tuna, a bit of chutney with the turkey—that made your tastebuds come to attention."

Even before she retired from Neiman Marcus, in 1969, the indefatigable Corbitt was expanding her legacy, lecturing all over the country and writing cookbooks—her first, *Helen Corbitt's Cookbook* (1957), had more than twenty-seven printings and sold more than three hundred thousand copies. Her cookbooks, now out of print, are a staple of every Texas cook's library. Worn-out copies, dog-eared and grease-splattered, are often rebound. Women who have cooked from her books all their lives light up with gratitude when her name is mentioned. "She taught me that I could entertain in a small apartment or in my kitchen without hired help," says a friend who used to have a catering business. ("Just throw a clean white cup towel over the dirty dishes in the sink!" Corbitt suggested in one of her lectures.)

Corbitt-trained cooks have their favorite recipes: the poppy-seed dressing for fruit salad; the pancake stack, ten to twelve very thin fourteen-inch pancakes, spread either with lemon-cream butter and hot blueberry sauce or with butter, maple syrup, and a little ham gravy, stacked, and sliced for serving like a pie; or perhaps the queen of desserts, caramel soufflé with English custard sauce. Of the latter, wrote Corbitt in *Cooks for Company*, "You may halve the recipe, but why? Regardless of how few guests you have, it will all be eaten."

The generous party spirit, awash in butter, cream cheese, eggs, and mayonnaise, that pervades her first two cookbooks (the second, *Helen Corbitt's Potluck*, was published in 1962) inevitably gave way to the low-cholesterol, low-cal recipe collections *Helen Corbitt Cooks for Looks* (1967) and *Helen Corbitt's Greenhouse Cookbook* (1979). Corbitt, like the rest of us, was fighting her own weight and cholesterol, and she refused to be limited to grapefruit and cottage cheese. Gone are the jaunty comments "Men will really love this" or "When you're feeling extravagant . . . ," but a number of good cooks swear by her simple roast chicken stuffed with grapes.

With missionary zeal, Corbitt shared her expertise. She taught cooking classes to benefit the Dallas Symphony, raising more than $150,000. She also taught a more intimate class of close friends and their daughters in the store, charging only for the food used in the demonstrations. The notes from those sessions were passed like heirlooms to a third generation. And she taught a rather exclusive cooking class for fourteen men on Wednesday nights in her duplex on University. Corbitt, who never married, clearly enjoyed her male following, and her cookbooks are most often dedicated to them. She liked that men asked questions and wanted to know the "why" of certain procedures. "She also liked that she could give us hell without worrying that she'd hurt our feelings," recalled one of her male pupils.

Helen Corbitt died of cancer in 1978. In the last year of her life, her good friend Father Don Fischer (now monsignor), then a young chaplain at the University of Dallas, took her the Eucharist daily. "It was a great gift to be able to bring spiritual food to such a lover of food," he said. "Even in her weakening condition, she always felt she should offer me something when I came to see her. I tried to beg off but finally said, 'Okay, but make it just something very simple.' She made me the best peanut-butter-and-jelly sandwich I've ever had. I know the bread was probably homemade. She spread it with butter, then a generous amount of peanut butter and marvelous preserves. I went away thinking that if that was what peanut butter and jelly was supposed to taste like, I had been a very deprived child."

In Texas, BC, most of us were. —*Prudence Mackintosh*

CHAPTER 5

On
Holiday

BY DAN SOLOMON

"The Road Goes on Forever and the Party Never Ends"

Robert Earl Keen wasn't thinking about food when he penned that classic refrain, but it does seem to capture the spirit of culinary adventure in this vast place. When I moved to the wildly diverse state of Texas from the wildly homogenous state of Indiana at eighteen, my learning curve was steep. Take the barbecue pilgrimage, for example. Had I ever driven miles out of my way for a plate of brisket? Nope. Or the Texas holiday table. Sure, my new state and I had turkey at Thanksgiving in common, but some of its other traditions were new to me, like tamales on Christmas Eve, which seemed downright exotic to this Hoosier. Black-eyed peas? I'm not sure I'd ever eaten any, and I'd definitely never eaten them for luck on New Year's Eve.

Part of being a Texan of the "wasn't born here but got here as fast as I could" variety is embracing what makes your new home special, and I quickly came to appreciate the food-focused celebrations that so unite folks who live here. There's one dish in particular that embodies holiday and party like no other, and that's tamales. When the offer first came, shortly after Thanksgiving, to "place an order" with someone's aunt or grandma, I felt like a true Texan. The store and restaurant varieties are just fine, but tamales are at their finest made at home, and preferably at a tamalada, a daylong, all-hands-on-deck, family-and-friends fiesta in which everyone gathers amid giant bowls of fragrant masa, simmering pots of chile-spiced meat, and ice-filled coolers of beer to take their place spreading, filling, and tying up little corn husk–wrapped packages. In fact, the tamalada soon became a tradition in my own home, and each December I fill my freezer with zip-top bags stuffed with pork, chicken, and bean-and-cheese tamales.

Just as rewarding as coming together to celebrate is exchanging the family table for a corner booth out on the highways and byways of this vast state. There's a certain restaurant that equals "road trip" in a Texan's mind. Yes, barbecue joints and Mexican food spots are popular options, but we are invariably drawn to a small-town cafe, the sort of place where regulars meet like clockwork over morning eggs, waitresses actually call you "hon," and red plastic glasses are continually refilled with too-sweet iced tea. The cuisine is almost uniformly brown—nary a green item to be seen except perhaps iceberg lettuce drenched in ranch dressing—because anything good can always be made better by an immersion in hot oil. Chicken-fried steak smothered in cream gravy is its apotheosis. You can't call yourself a Texan until you've eaten your way through the country cafes that lie waiting at the end of every off-ramp or pulled over at a diner that looks as if it might be serving up something special. As *Texas Monthly* once put it, "The image of the small-town Texas cafe exerts a powerful pull on our collective unconscious.... Such places carry the promise of that ever-elusive 'simpler time,' when communities were bound by shared stories, pan-fried chicken, and hot coffee."

I know that these traditions are deeply meaningful to the Texans who've shared them with me and my fellow transplants. And though it's been said that the zeal of the convert is the strongest, I'm not entirely sure that's true; my childhood holiday memories are of my Polish grandmother rolling out ruskie dough, not masa. But I'm certain that the legendary Texas hospitality that I've been so lucky to enjoy has never been more apparent—or important—than when I've been invited to a friend's holiday table or handed a well-worn menu at a roadside cafe. The celebrations and adventures that are so important to native-born Texans have become my own, and I'm all the richer for it.

Smoked Turkey

Turkey breast is a staple of Texas barbecue, but a whole smoked turkey is a special occasion, perfect for the winter holidays. Smoking is one of the best ways to cook a turkey: the low-and-slow nature of this method keeps the meat moist, and the smoke adds tons of flavor to what can be, in the wrong hands, a bland bird. Bonus? Smoking your bird means the oven's free for tons of sides and pies. And who doesn't want more pie?!

1 turkey

1 tablespoon salt for every 3 pounds of turkey (a 12-pound bird gets 4 tablespoons, for example)

1½ teaspoons ground black pepper for every 3 pounds of turkey (a 12-pounder gets 6 teaspoons)

Special equipment: smoker

The day before cooking, spatchcock the turkey: using poultry or kitchen shears, carefully cut down both sides of the backbone and remove. (You may save the backbone for stock to make gravy, if you wish.) Flip the turkey over on a cutting board, and place the palms of your hands at the top center of the breast. Putting your weight behind it, press down hard on the breastbone—you should feel or hear two pops. Larger birds may be trickier to spatchcock, but often butchers will do this step for you if you ask.

Heat a smoker to 325°F.

Place the turkey skin-side up directly on the smoker grate and close the lid. The bird will take 12 to 13 minutes per pound to cook (12 pounds will take about 2½ hours). The turkey is done when the internal temperature of the breast reaches 165°F; the legs can handle going a bit hotter than that before they dry out.

Use heatproof gloves, tongs, or a pair of large, hefty spatulas to carefully remove the turkey from the smoker to a cutting board. Cover with foil and let rest for 20 to 30 minutes. The bigger the turkey, the longer it needs to rest.

Carve the turkey and serve.

Cranberry Chutney

This recipe comes from home cook and *Texas Monthly* reader Meena Habbu, of Colleyville, who incorporates cranberries with classic Indian chutney flavors for a tart-sweet-spicy condiment. She says, "We typically eat this with any bread, but it's especially good with a turkey sandwich after Thanksgiving!"

Makes about 2 cups

½ teaspoon fenugreek seeds

½ cup dried, shredded unsweetened coconut

1 pound fresh cranberries

Salt

⅓ cup brown sugar

1 teaspoon cayenne pepper (or less, if you don't like spice)

1 tablespoon vegetable or canola oil

½ teaspoon black mustard seeds

¼ teaspoon asafoetida (also known as hing)

In a large skillet, lightly toast the fenugreek seeds over medium heat until fragrant. Add the coconut and toast, stirring, until light brown, about 2 minutes. Remove from the heat and set aside.

In a blender, combine the cranberries, a pinch of salt, the brown sugar, and cayenne with the toasted fenugreek and coconut and blend until they form a paste.

In the same skillet, heat the oil over medium heat. Add the mustard seeds and cook until they sputter. Turn off the heat. Stir in the asafoetida and cranberry paste, season with salt, and serve.

In Defense of Just Eating Your Dang Thanksgiving Dinner at Luby's

Maybe you're the type of person who watches videos of people deep-frying turkeys year-round, tucking them away on a Pinterest board full of Thanksgiving inspiration. Maybe you harvest your own cranberries to make a homemade sauce that bears no resemblance to the gelatinous, can-shaped blobs that define the holiday condiment in the popular imagination. Maybe you've got an overstuffed binder full of ideas for how to make the perfect ham glaze (Tabasco + grape jelly + brown mustard?) that you wait all year to deploy. Maybe you get up at dawn on Thanksgiving to hand-knead the dough for your famous rolls, risen twice before baking, with a pot of boiling sweet potatoes raring to go.

If so, cool. If not, let's get right to it: The holidays are stressful. They're a lot of work. Thanksgiving requires some degree of sacrifice just a month before another, even *more* stressful holiday season for most Americans. If you're not cooking Thanksgiving dinner, you're probably traveling. If you're not traveling, you're enduring the company of uncles and cousins and friends-of-uncles and friends-of-cousins you'd rather not see, hoping that the football games are competitive enough to help you tune out political rants from people who, if not for a shared connection on your family tree, you'd probably cross the street to avoid.

At the same time, Thanksgiving dinner *is* a tradition. There's something exceedingly lonely about sitting out a holiday entirely, boiling a pot of pasta on the stovetop to eat with butter and garlic powder with the lights off, while at homes across the nation, everyone else sits down to a holy storm of turkey, potatoes, cornbread dressing, and green bean casserole.

For those of us who want to experience the good parts of Thanksgiving while also being able to avoid the parts of the holiday that spike our cortisol levels, there is an option. It's called Luby's. Luby's occupies a special place in the hearts of many Texans, who collectively breathed a sigh of relief when the beleaguered company found a buyer in 2021 for thirty-two of its locations. The LuAnn Platter was a staple of a lot of people's childhoods, a place where they watched their grandparents eat liver and onions while they enjoyed chicken-fried chicken and mac and cheese. It's a place that fills many of us with various feelings, and none of 'em are bad.

And they serve Thanksgiving dinner there too. On years when financial, chronal, or geographic realities made a trip out of town to spend Thanksgiving with family impossible, I've looked for a way to have a Thanksgiving experience on my own terms, and Luby's has been an above-average choice. There aren't a lot of restaurants open on Thanksgiving—IHOP, Denny's, Waffle House, and the like stay open, but who wants pancakes for Thanksgiving dinner?—but Luby's would rate highly regardless of the competition.

The appeal of Luby's on Thanksgiving is largely that it serves Thanksgiving dinner every other day of the year too. It doesn't need to gussy up its menu in an attempt to offer a special Thanksgiving feast. Roast turkey, mac and cheese, sweet potatoes, and rolls are a perfectly acceptable Luby's meal on any given Thursday. It's not veering off into unconventional territory; rather, it's the occupant of a perfect Venn diagram between "Thanksgiving" and "casual dining."

There are times in a person's life when a Luby's Thanksgiving might not be the ideal way to celebrate. When there are young kids involved, or aging parents, or other responsibilities that make attending—or hosting—a Thanksgiving dinner in a family home the most responsible way to treat the holiday, then even the chain's Thanksgiving special (turkey, dressing, two sides, and dessert for $11.49) is unlikely to provide an acceptable alternative. But if you spend a couple years celebrating the holiday with a few friends at Luby's, where someone else has to do all the cooking and cleaning up and the only loud uncles in the building are not your own relatives, you might find that, when it's time to celebrate Thanksgiving, that $11.49 special sounds pretty good.—*Dan Solomon*

Grilled Lamb Rib Chops with Minted Vinegar Dipping Sauce

About an hour south of Abilene is tiny Talpa, home to the restaurant and hotel Rancho Loma. Run by Robert and Laurie Williamson, Rancho Loma is a relaxing destination, a place to unplug, gaze at stars unobstructed by city light, and enjoy dishes like these grilled lamb chops. Laurie likes to serve the sauce in individual mismatched bowls: teacups, sake cups, ramen spoons, and any other attractive vessels that might be on hand.

Serves 4

For the sauce

⅓ cup white wine vinegar

½ cup sugar

½ cup fresh mint leaves

For the lamb

12 single lamb rib chops, frenched

1 garlic clove, cut in half

1 teaspoon dried thyme

Salt and ground black pepper

TO MAKE THE SAUCE:

Combine the vinegar and sugar in a small saucepan and cook over medium heat until the sugar is dissolved. Stir in the mint and let the sauce cool. Strain and set aside.

TO MAKE THE LAMB:

Pat the chops dry, then rub them with garlic, sprinkle with the thyme, and season with salt and pepper. Grill over direct medium-high heat for 1½ to 2 minutes per side, depending on how well-done you like your lamb. Serve with the dipping sauce.

Soup Joumou

Houston chef Jonny Rhodes, who garnered national acclaim for his now-closed Indigo, went to Haiti in 2019, which is where he first had this colorful, vegetable-studded beef stew. "I watched a lady cook this entire dish over live fire," he says, "and it required so much finesse, so much skill. Not to mention the heat was really hot!" Though it's traditionally served on January 1 to commemorate Haitian Independence Day, Rhodes often serves it for his family all autumn long, when the squash necessary to make it grows in "overabundance" on his farm.

Serves 8

1½ pounds oxtails

1¼ cups distilled white vinegar, divided

1 cup epis (available online and in specialty stores)

Juice of 3 limes

2 tablespoons adobo seasoning

1 pound chuck stew meat

4 quarts beef broth

1 pound honeynut or butternut squash, peeled and chopped

1 pound kabocha squash, peeled and chopped

1½ pounds Yukon Gold potatoes

4 carrots, sliced

½ pound green cabbage, cored and thinly sliced

1 large yellow onion, diced

2 celery hearts or 4 lovage leaves, minced

1 leek, white and tender green parts, diced

1 shallot, diced

2 purple top turnips with their greens; turnips diced, greens chopped

½ cup chopped fresh flat-leaf parsley

5 tablespoons garlic oil

2 to 3 tablespoons unsalted butter

4 tablespoons everything seasoning, for garnish

Special equipment: smoker

Rinse the oxtails with ½ cup of the vinegar, then place in a colander and rinse with water. Prepare a smoker to 225°F and smoke the oxtails for 2 hours.

In a large bowl, combine the epis, lime juice, and adobo seasoning. Rinse the stew meat with ½ cup of the remaining vinegar, then place in a colander and rinse with water. Add the smoked oxtails and stew meat to the marinade and let marinate at least 30 minutes but preferably overnight in the refrigerator.

Heat 5 cups of the broth in a very large stockpot over medium heat. Add the marinated beef and oxtails, cover, and simmer for about 45 minutes. Add the squash to the pot on top of the beef, cover, and return to a simmer. Cook until the squash is fork-tender, about 25 minutes.

Using tongs or a slotted spoon, transfer the squash to a blender. Add 4 cups of the remaining broth to the blender and puree until smooth. Return the puree to the pot and bring to a simmer.

Add the potatoes, carrots, cabbage, onion, celery hearts, leek, shallot, turnips, parsley, and remaining broth. Simmer, uncovered, until the vegetables are tender, 30 to 35 minutes. Add the garlic oil, butter, and remaining ¼ cup vinegar. Reduce the heat to medium-low and simmer until the beef is very tender, 15 to 20 minutes more. Taste and adjust the seasonings. Divide the soup among bowls, sprinkle with the everything seasoning, and serve with bread alongside.

Pork Tamales

There's a reason tamales are typically a special-occasion food, served during celebrations and holidays, and often assembled amid the convivial chaos of an assembly line–style tamalada: they're exhausting to make. But the results are so fluffy, fragrant, and delicious that you won't regret a single bit of all that chile-prepping, husk-cleaning, meat-shredding, and dough-spreading. So whip up some margaritas, warm a pot of queso on the stove, and invite twenty or so of your best friends to come help. They'll be happy to dive right in knowing they'll get to take home the fruits of their labor.

Makes 12 to 20, depending on size

For the wrappers

1 package dried corn husks

For the pork

1½ pounds pork butt (shoulder), trimmed and cut into large cubes

½ white onion, peeled

2 garlic cloves, peeled

2 teaspoons kosher salt

¼ teaspoon coarsely ground black pepper

For the chile paste

3 ancho chiles, stems and seeds removed

3 guajillo chiles, stems and seeds removed

1½ tablespoons lard (see Notes)

3 garlic cloves, peeled

1 teaspoon kosher salt

½ teaspoon ground cumin

¼ teaspoon ground black pepper

For the masa

½ cup lard, slightly chilled

1 teaspoon baking powder

1 pound coarse-ground masa for tamales (see Notes)

Broth reserved from the pork butt (see above), cooled and skimmed of fat

Salt

TO PREP THE CORN HUSKS:

Place a big handful of corn husks in a large bowl and cover with hot water; use a plate or heavy object to keep them submerged for about an hour.

TO MAKE THE PORK:

Put the pork, onion, garlic, salt, and pepper in a large pot and cover with water. Bring to a boil over high heat, then reduce the heat to maintain a simmer and cook for 1½ hours, periodically skimming and discarding the foam that rises to the top.

Allow to cool, then shred the meat with your fingers or two forks positioned back-to-back. Set the meat aside and strain and refrigerate the broth.

TO MAKE THE CHILE PASTE:

In a medium heavy skillet, fry the ancho and guajillo chiles in 1½ teaspoons of the lard until fragrant, about 30 seconds. (You can also dry-roast them in a cast-iron pan.) Place the chiles in a bowl, cover with boiling water (about 2 cups), and let them soak for 15 to 20 minutes.

Add the soaked chiles to a blender along with 1 cup of the soaking liquid, plus the garlic, salt, cumin, and black pepper. Blend, adding additional liquid a little at a time if necessary, until it becomes a fine paste.

(cont.)

Melt the remaining 1 tablespoon lard in the skillet and fry the paste (watch out for splatter) for a minute or so, until it turns dark and fragrant. Add ¾ cup of the remaining chile liquid and simmer for about 15 minutes, until thick and glossy.

Add ¼ cup of the chile paste to the pork. Taste and add salt or more chile paste to your taste. You can also reserve a bit of the remaining chile paste for the masa.

At this point you can refrigerate the pork mixture and chile paste overnight or continue with the recipe.

TO MAKE THE MASA:

Using an electric mixer, beat the lard with the baking powder at medium-high speed until light and somewhat fluffy, about 1 minute. Continue beating as you add the masa, in 3 or 4 additions. You can add a bit of the chile paste here if you like.

With the mixer on, slowly add ½ cup of the pork broth and continue to beat until the batter has the consistency of cake batter or hummus. Season with salt.

TO MAKE THE TAMALES:

Pick out some husks of equal size and dry thoroughly. Tear a few more husks into narrow strips for tying the tamales. Put a dollop of batter in the middle of the larger end of each husk, with the narrow end pointing away from you. Spread into an even layer, leaving about ½ inch of border on the sides and bottom and at least 2 inches at the top.

Put a couple of spoonfuls of pork down the center of the batter, lengthwise, then bring the long sides of the husk together and fold one over the other. Fold the bottom point upward and secure the tamal by tying with a strip of husk. Repeat with the rest of the husks until you have used up all the filling.

Add water to a stockpot and insert a steamer basket (the water should not reach the bottom of the basket). Line the bottom of the steamer with a few more corn husks and place the tamales upright; you can use wadded-up pieces of aluminum foil to prop them up. Put a few more husks on top of the tamales and bring the water to a boil.

Cover the pot and steam over medium heat for 1 to 1½ hours (replenish the water occasionally and keep it boiling). The tamales are done when their husks pull away from the filling cleanly. Let sit off the heat for a few minutes before serving.

Notes: Instead of lard, you can use your preferred fat; for the chile paste and the masa, we used the light brown, refrigerated manteca found in the meat department of most Mexican markets. You'll want to prepare the masa at least an hour before you assemble your tamales. Masa for tamales is an already-prepared dough, usually in a 5-pound bag, found in Mexican markets. You can also use dried masa harina, which you'll need to prepare following the directions on the package.

The Texanist is *Texas Monthly* senior editor David Courtney.

THE TEXANIST ON

What's the Deal with Tamales and Christmas?

Among all the world's gastronomic traditions, is there one that is more delectable than that of Mexico? The Texanist, an admittedly rabid devotee of most all foodstuffs originating south of the border, is certain that there is not. One of the stars of the Mexican kitchen—as well as the Tex-Mex kitchen—is the tamale, a delicious treat made with masa and a filling of the tamalera's (tamale maker) choosing. There's beef, chicken, bean, bean and cheese, squash, sweet corn, and on and on and on. The tamale options are infinite. The Texanist's favorite is the classic pork variety. Glistening and slippery, they are the quintessential tamale, and the Texanist is known to devour fistfuls of the slick little devils throughout the year. Mmm-mmm! Washed down with a Big Red or some cold Mexican suds, there's nothing like it.

The debt of gratitude for the invention of the tamale is owed to the great Mesoamerican cultures of millennia past. The Aztec, Maya, Mixtec, Olmec, Toltec, and Zapotec all took nourishment from the small banana leaf or corn husk–wrapped packets of goodness, and each passed down their tamale customs through the generations. Interestingly, though, none of these ancient cultures were known to have celebrated Christmas. Indeed, some of them predated the birth of Christianity and none of

them had even heard of Christmas before the Europeans arrived in the early sixteenth century. These peoples did observe their own traditions and celebrations—some of which involved sacrificial offerings (sometimes human) to their deities. There's a theory that has such gruesome gifts being replaced, at some point, with a much more civilized option—tamales. The likes of Xochipilli, Tonacatecuhtli, and Ah Kinchil must have been very grateful for the change. The Texanist knows he certainly would have been were he an ancient god.

The thinking is that over time tamales became associated with special occasions, and as the Mexican population was eventually Christianized, the tradition was transferred to the most important holiday on the Christian calendar. Which is why, come the holiday season, it is common for Mexican, Mexican-Texan, and Mexican-American families and friends to gather in kitchens big and small for annual tamaladas, or tamale-making parties. The fruits of such gatherings, the dozens upon dozens of delicious tamales, are then divvied up and dispersed to friends, coworkers, and loved ones far and wide. Christmastime in Texas means it's also tamale time in Texas. Can the Texanist get a great big hallelujah?

Buttermilk-Fried Chicken Liver and Caramelized Onion Po'boys

As the saying goes, Michelle Wallace (pictured on page 159) didn't grow up in Texas, but she got here as fast as she could. The St. Louis native says that when she arrived, "The food scene just took hold of me." She is now the executive chef at Gatlin's BBQ, in Houston, and a self-proclaimed sandwich queen, and she offers these chicken liver po'boys for all manner of celebrations. "I grew up eating liver and onions," she says. "It's actually one of my favorite things." A bacon-apple spread adds something sweet and salty, Havarti adds creaminess, and arugula cuts through it all.

Makes 4 sandwiches

For the caramelized onions

3 tablespoons grapeseed oil

2 medium yellow onions, sliced (3 to 4 cups)

1 dried bay leaf

For the bacon-apple chutney

1 pound bacon, diced

1 medium shallot, finely diced

5 garlic cloves, minced

½ serrano chile, stem removed, finely diced (for a spicier chutney, use the whole chile)

1 pound apples, peeled, cored, and diced (a mix of Granny Smith and Honeycrisp works nicely)

2 tablespoons brown sugar

1 tablespoon honey

1 tablespoon sherry vinegar

Juice of 1 lemon

Salt

2 teaspoons chopped fresh sage

TO MAKE THE CARAMELIZED ONIONS:

Heat the oil in a large sauté pan over medium heat. Add the onions and bay leaf and turn the heat down to medium-low. Let the onions slowly caramelize until they're a light golden color, 25 to 35 minutes. Remove from the pan and discard the bay leaf. Use immediately or cool, place in a container, and refrigerate.

TO MAKE THE BACON-APPLE CHUTNEY:

Put the bacon in a large cold skillet. Turn the heat to medium and cook the bacon, stirring occasionally, until golden brown and just crisp. Remove from the pan with a slotted spoon to a paper towel–lined plate. Reserve about 4 tablespoons of bacon fat in the pan and discard the rest.

Add the shallot to the fat in the pan and cook for 2 minutes, then add the garlic and chile and cook for 2 more minutes. Add the apples and cook just until the apples have softened, about 10 minutes.

Add the brown sugar, honey, vinegar, and lemon juice to the pan and simmer until the mixture has thickened, 8 to 10 minutes. Taste and add salt if needed. Add the sage and stir to combine.

Let the mixture cool for about 5 minutes, then transfer to a food processor and pulse 8 to 10 times, until the chutney is coarse but spreadable. Refrigerate until ready to use.

For the chicken livers

1 cup buttermilk

2 tablespoons hot sauce

2 pounds chicken livers, cleaned and trimmed (see Note)

1½ cups all-purpose flour

½ cup cornstarch

1 tablespoon Cajun seasoning, plus additional seasoning for dusting the fried livers

1 teaspoon granulated garlic

1 teaspoon paprika

1 teaspoon ground black pepper

1 teaspoon kosher salt

2 eggs

Canola oil, for frying

For the po'boys

4 (5-inch-long) French loaves

Bacon-Apple Chutney

8 slices Havarti cheese

Chicken Livers

Caramelized Onions

2 cups arugula leaves

TO MAKE THE CHICKEN LIVERS:

In a large bowl, whisk together the buttermilk and hot sauce. Add the chicken livers, stir to coat, then refrigerate, covered, for at least 2 and no more than 12 hours.

In a shallow pan or pie tin, combine the flour, cornstarch, Cajun seasoning, granulated garlic, paprika, black pepper, and salt. Set aside.

Drain the livers in a colander and place in a bowl. Crack the eggs into a small bowl and whisk, then pour over the livers. Dredge each liver in the seasoned flour and place on a parchment-lined sheet pan.

Pour 1½ inches of oil into a large, heavy skillet. Line a sheet pan with paper towels. Heat the oil over medium-high heat until it reaches 350°F. Working in batches, place the floured livers into the oil and fry, turning occasionally, until golden brown and crisp, 3 to 4 minutes per side. Transfer to the paper towel–lined sheet pan and dust with Cajun seasoning.

TO MAKE THE PO'BOYS:

Split the French bread horizontally and spread 2 to 3 tablespoons of chutney across the bottom of each loaf. Top with 2 slices of cheese. Add 2 to 3 livers to each loaf, then top with a few tablespoons of caramelized onions. Finish each sandwich with ½ cup arugula.

Note: Use a sharp pair of scissors or a paring knife to remove any connective tissue or sinewy bits clinging to the livers. Chicken livers require at least 2 hours (and up to 12 hours) to marinate. Also, because of their high water content, they have a tendency to splatter a bit when you fry them. A fryer with a lid, or even a pot lid, should help.

Charred Okra and Onions with Lemon-Anchovy Vinaigrette

"When people say they don't like okra," says Michelle Wallace, "typically it's because of the slime." This dish takes the slime out of the equation: by charring the okra—along with some sweet cipollini onions—you get a nice crisp texture. This dish is the perfect accompaniment to her Buttermilk-Fried Chicken Liver and Caramelized Onion Po'boys (page 174).

Serves 6

For the lemon-anchovy vinaigrette

4 anchovy fillets, minced

3 garlic cloves, minced

Juice of 1 lemon

1 teaspoon Dijon mustard

½ teaspoon honey

¾ cup grapeseed oil

½ teaspoon ground black pepper

Salt

For the okra and onions

2 pounds okra, trimmed and cut in half lengthwise

2 tablespoons grapeseed oil, divided, plus more as needed

Salt and ground black pepper

8 to 10 cipollini onions, cut in half

Lemon-Anchovy Vinaigrette

¼ cup chopped fresh flat-leaf parsley

TO MAKE THE LEMON-ANCHOVY VINAIGRETTE:

In a medium bowl, whisk together the minced anchovies, garlic, lemon juice, mustard, and honey. While whisking continuously, slowly add the oil. Add the black pepper and season with salt. Taste and add more salt if necessary. Refrigerate until needed.

TO MAKE THE OKRA AND ONIONS:

In a large bowl, toss the halved okra with 1 tablespoon of the oil and a large pinch each of salt and black pepper. Set aside.

Heat a large cast-iron skillet over medium-high heat until hot. Working in batches, cook the okra, cut-side down, in a single layer, allowing to char for 3 to 4 minutes before flipping. Cook for an additional minute, then remove from the pan and place on a serving platter. (If needed, add additional oil as you cook.)

After the okra is charred, repeat the process with the onions. Toss them in the rest of the oil, adding a large pinch each of salt and pepper. Add to the skillet cut-side down and cook for 3 minutes, then flip and cook for an additional minute.

Transfer the onions to the serving platter, drizzle with the vinaigrette (you may not need all of it), and sprinkle with the parsley.

New Year's Day Black-Eyed Peas

Eating black-eyed peas for good fortune and prosperity in the new year is very much a Southern tradition, one that Texans have adopted with gusto. How the association between pea consumption and good luck came to be is hard to determine, but who could argue with a pot of creamy legumes aswim in a garlicky broth brightened by aromatic herbs and enriched with smoky ham hock?

Serves about 4

12 ounces fresh or dried black-eyed, purple hull, or other type of crowder peas

2 tablespoons bacon fat or butter

1 yellow onion, diced (about 1 cup)

4 garlic cloves, minced

2 celery stalks, diced (about ½ cup)

2 carrots, diced (about ½ cup)

1 jalapeño chile, stem and seeds removed, minced

2 cups chicken stock

1 bone-in smoked ham hock, about 1 pound

1 sprig thyme

1 sprig rosemary

1 teaspoon salt, plus more to taste

½ teaspoon ground black pepper, plus more to taste

2 tablespoons apple cider vinegar

Put the peas in a strainer and rinse thoroughly with water. If using dried peas, soak overnight in enough water to cover by 2 to 3 inches. The next day, drain the peas.

In a large heavy-bottomed pot or Dutch oven, melt the bacon fat or butter over medium heat. Add the onion, garlic, celery, carrots, and chile. Cook until soft, about 3 minutes.

Add the peas, chicken stock, ham hock, thyme, rosemary, salt, and pepper. Stir to combine, bring to a boil, then reduce the heat to maintain a simmer. If using fresh peas, cook for 1 hour and 15 minutes to 1 hour and 30 minutes; if using dried peas, cook for 1 hour and 30 minutes to 2 hours. When done, the peas should be tender, not chalky or mushy. Turn off the heat.

Use tongs to remove the ham hock to a cutting board. Remove the thyme and rosemary stems as well. When the ham is cool enough to handle, remove the meat from the bone and chop into bite-size pieces. Add them back into the pot. Add the vinegar. Taste and add salt and pepper as needed.

If desired, serve with collards, rice and/or cornbread, and the hot sauce of your choice.

ODE TO
Chicken-Fried Steak

Chicken-fried steak is the great equalizer. Its very preparation—the energetic pounding with a mallet, the vigorous dredging in flour, the immersion in splattering hot grease—puts all who make it on the same messy plane. It is also democratic to the core: The tenderized steak at its center can be as high-grade as a rib eye or as lowly as a round steak. And then there's its broad appeal. In small towns, the best chicken-fried steak is found at the cafe with the most pickup trucks parked out front. But big-city owners of Cadillacs and Lexuses relish the dish just as much. Cowboys, hairdressers, bankers, lawyers—is there anyone who can resist that golden crunchy crust, that fork-tender beef, or that luxurious blanket of peppery white gravy? Chicken-fried steak is our shared birthright.—*June Naylor*

Chicken-Fried Steak with Cream Gravy

Beaten, floured, and bathed in hot fat, chicken-fried steak is a Texas treasure, a miracle of ingenuity that some think evolved from schnitzel-loving German immigrants and others from scrappy chuck-wagon cooks struggling to address the comestible shortcomings of trail-weary longhorn cattle. Sadly, a CFS nowadays is often a factory-formed and -breaded meat patty of entirely suspect origins, frozen solid and sent hurtling down the highway in a semi. Make this at home and you'll quickly remember what a real CFS is supposed to taste like.

Serves 4

4 cube steaks

2 teaspoons salt

2 teaspoons ground black pepper

1 teaspoon paprika

2¼ cups all-purpose flour

1 egg

1 cup buttermilk

1 cup vegetable oil, plus more if needed

2 cups whole milk

Season the steaks with 1 teaspoon of the salt and 1 teaspoon of the pepper.

In a shallow dish, whisk together the remaining 1 teaspoon salt and 1 teaspoon pepper, the paprika, and 2 cups of the flour.

In a second shallow dish, whisk together the egg and buttermilk.

One at a time, dip the steaks into the flour, pressing down to make sure all exposed surfaces are coated. Dip the steak into the egg mixture, and then back into the flour mixture. Set aside on a sheet pan.

Pour the oil into a large skillet (you should have about ½ inch of oil) and heat over medium-high heat. Fry the steaks until golden, about 3 minutes per side, and remove from the oil to drain on paper towels. Let rest while you make the gravy.

Pour all but ¼ cup oil out of the pan. Whisk ¼ cup flour into the oil and cook briefly, stirring (you don't want it to darken, you just want to take the raw edge off the flour), about 1 minute. Slowly pour in the milk, whisking as you go, and bring to a simmer. Simmer until thickened, taste for seasoning, and serve over the steaks.

Fried Okra

Our Texas accent skews decidedly Southern when it comes to okra. We like those fuzzy little pods cooked all kinds of ways, especially coated in a crispy, crackly crust. A simple bath in milk, a romp in a bowl of flour and cornmeal, and a dip in hot oil are all that's needed to render the mucilaginous veggie into the stuff of dreams.

Serves 6 as a side

Vegetable oil, for frying

½ cup whole milk

2 cups all-purpose flour

1 cup cornmeal

Salt and ground black pepper

1 pound fresh okra, stems removed and sliced into ½-inch rounds

In a large cast-iron skillet, heat about an inch of oil to 350°F.

Pour the milk into a shallow bowl; in another bowl, stir together the flour and cornmeal and season with salt and pepper (feel free to add other seasonings—Cajun seasoning, cayenne, garlic salt—in addition to or instead of the salt and pepper).

In batches, dip the okra in the milk, then dredge in the flour mixture until well coated, letting any excess flour fall through your fingers.

Using a slotted spoon or a spider, lower the okra into the hot oil and fry for 2 to 3 minutes, stirring occasionally, until golden brown, then drain on paper towels.

Onion Rings

Named for its optimal planting date, the 1015 onion is a Rio Grande Valley all-star. Some claim it's mild enough to eat raw, like an apple, but for a minimalist preparation that still glorifies its natural beauty and taste, you can't do much better than onion rings (what defenseless vegetable doesn't benefit from a quick dip in hot oil?). The symbiosis of sweet, warm onion and crunchy, salty batter makes those golden hoops the ultimate showcase for the singular 1015.

Serves 4 to 6

2 cups all-purpose flour

2 teaspoons salt

1 teaspoon ground black pepper

3 eggs, beaten

1 cup buttermilk

1 (12-ounce) can beer

2 Texas 1015 onions (or any sweet onion), cut crosswise into ¾-inch-thick rings

Vegetable oil, for frying

Ranch dressing, for dipping

Preheat the oven to 200°F, or use the "keep warm" setting, if your oven has one.

Set out a wire rack, as well as a sheet pan fitted with another wire rack.

In a shallow dish (a pie pan works well), combine the flour, salt, and pepper.

In another shallow dish, whisk together the eggs, buttermilk, and beer.

Separate the onion cross-sections into individual rings. One ring at a time, dip in the egg mixture, then the flour mixture, then the egg mixture, then the flour mixture. Put the ring on a wire rack while you finish coating all the rings.

Heat 2 inches of vegetable oil in a large, heavy-bottomed pan to 375°F. Working in batches, fry the onion rings until golden, about 5 minutes. Remove the onion rings to the sheet pan fitted with the wire rack and keep warm in the oven as you work. Once all the onion rings are fried, sprinkle with salt and serve with ranch dressing.

Fried Jalapeños

Stuffed with cheese, the fried jalapeño is a scrapper in an otherwise peaceable playground of happy-hour chow like mozzarella sticks and potato skins. Even its various names—poppers, rattlesnake eggs, torpedoes—portend bodily insult of some kind. But it also unites a few of Texans' favorite things in one fiery, addictive, delectable morsel that those lacking our born-and-bred fortitude may want to steer clear of.

Makes 1 dozen

⅓ cup all-purpose flour

½ teaspoon ground cumin

½ teaspoon granulated garlic

1 teaspoon salt, plus more to taste

½ teaspoon ground black pepper

1 egg

1 cup whole milk

1 cup unseasoned bread crumbs or cornmeal

1 (26-ounce) can whole pickled jalapeños, about 12 (you may want to experiment with different brands, as some hold up to slicing and stuffing better than others; we liked Trappey's and Don Lupe)

½ pound block Muenster cheese (or any easy-melting cheese), shredded or cut into fat matchsticks

½ cup cream cheese (optional)

Vegetable oil, for frying

In a shallow bowl, combine the flour with the cumin, granulated garlic, salt, and pepper. In another shallow bowl, whisk the egg with the milk. Place the bread crumbs in a third bowl.

Make a slit in the side of the pickled jalapeños from top to bottom, being careful not to cut all the way through. Pull off the stems with your fingers and remove the ribs and seeds (this is a little tricky but gets easier with practice; a grapefruit spoon is helpful). You may want to wear disposable gloves for this step.

Stuff each pickled jalapeño with Muenster (amount will depend on size) and a dab of cream cheese, if desired, pressing it in and bringing the edges together as best you can.

Dunk each stuffed pickled jalapeño in the egg wash, then roll in the seasoned flour, coating thoroughly, and place on a parchment paper–lined plate or tray.

Heat 2 to 3 inches of oil in a large heavy-bottomed pot or cast-iron pan to 350°F.

Return the floured pickled jalapeños to the egg wash and then roll in the bread crumbs.

Fry the pickled jalapeños, a few at a time, until they're golden brown, about 5 minutes for bread crumbs and 6 minutes for cornmeal. Remove them to a paper towel–lined plate or tray and sprinkle with salt.

Serve shamelessly with ranch dressing, a splendid counterpoint to the piquant heat of the jalapeño.

Note: If you are making several batches, the fried jalapeños may be held in a 200°F oven until ready to serve.

Strawberry Fried Pies

The fried pie, a warm half-moon of flaky pastry, its crimped edges barely containing a molten core of sweet fruit, is no newfangled novelty à la the state fair but a fixture in the annals of Texas culinary history. Traditionally scraped together from leftover dough, plentiful fat, and less plentiful but easily preserved fruit, the fried pie has been many things to many people—a welcome guest at chuck wagon suppers, a coveted addition to school lunch pails, a sugar-scented memory of Grandma's kitchen.

Makes about a dozen 3-inch pies

For the dough (can also use store-bought rolled pie dough, enough for two crusts)

2 cups all-purpose flour, plus more for dusting

1 teaspoon sugar

½ teaspoon salt

1 cup (2 sticks) cold unsalted butter, diced

Ice water

For the filling

½ cup sugar

2 tablespoons cornstarch

Juice of ½ lemon

1 pint fresh strawberries, hulled and diced

Vegetable oil, for frying

TO MAKE THE DOUGH:

In a large bowl, whisk together the flour, sugar, and salt. Use a pastry cutter or a fork to cut the butter into the flour, working it until the largest chunks of butter are the size of a pea.

Add ice water a tablespoon or two at a time, working it in with a wooden spoon, until the dough comes together (about ¼ cup water). Briefly knead in the bowl, then form into a round disk. Wrap in plastic wrap and refrigerate while you make the filling.

TO MAKE THE FILLING:

Combine the sugar, cornstarch, lemon juice, and ¾ cup water in a medium saucepan. Heat over medium-low heat until thickened, about 3 minutes. Remove from the heat and fold in the strawberries.

TO MAKE THE FRIED PIES:

Split the pie dough into 12 golf ball–size pieces and use your hands to roll them into balls. Flour a work surface and use a lightly floured rolling pin to roll them into 3-inch circles.

Place about 1½ tablespoons of the filling in the middle of each round. Dip a finger in water and use it to wet the edge of the circle of dough, then fold it in half. Use a fork to crimp the edges of the dough together.

In a deep, wide pan, heat about 4 inches of oil to 350°F. A few at a time, fry the pies until golden, about 2 minutes. Use a slotted spoon to remove the pies to a paper towel–lined tray. Let cool for a few minutes before serving.

CHAPTER 6

Rise
and
Shine

BY CHRISTIAN WALLACE

Breakfasts for Bloody Mary Mornings

I'm sure Willie would agree: of the dairy meals, breakfast tends to be the most democratic. Though you can certainly find urban Texans sipping bottomless mimosas over pork belly Benedicts on weekend mornings, most of the time breakfast is a straightforward, down-home affair. Hearty, simple, delicious. Still, Texans are spoiled for choice. "Home" has meant many things to many Texans over the centuries, and as such we start our days (if not in our own home) at eateries that range from hole-in-the-wall taquerias and fragrant Czech-style bakeries to wood-paneled diners and bustling chicken-and-waffle joints.

You'd have to go all the way back to the chuck wagon for my favorite breakfast dish, biscuits and gravy. We Texans share that doughy devotion with Southerners, of course, but I like to think they are a Texan's birthright. I was lucky enough to grow up in West Texas, where plates of flaky, buttery biscuits smothered in meaty gravy were served at the kitchen table, at school, and in practically every cafe worth its table salt. My favorite version of the dish is my grandpa's. A horse trainer by trade, he could mix up a batch of dough as easily as he could swing a leg over the saddle. Sometimes he'd build a small fire and bake the bread in a Dutch oven over the coals. That's how my great-granny, a ranch wife who fed a whole outfit of hungry cowboys day in and day out, had taught him. A biscuit of my grandpa's caliber can be downright sacred. To paraphrase a favorite Texas expression, "The higher the biscuit, the closer to God."

There's another pillowy pastry, though, that inspires near fanaticism within the state and intense curiosity outside it: the kolache. I was first exposed to the wonders of sweet kolaches—and their savory cousins, klobasniky—when I moved to the Hill Country for college. Central Texas was the favored destination for Czechs immigrating to the state in the mid-1800s, and we have them to thank for these warm, yeasty, fruit-filled works of art. There was a time, not so long ago, when they were served almost exclusively in communities with a strong Czech background. But these days both kolaches and klobasniky (see page 204 for the difference) are offered, alongside doughnuts and cinnamon rolls and muffins, all across the state, from Perryton to McAllen. And as they've grown in popularity, brilliant regional variations have popped up, such as the klobasniky stuffed with mouthwatering boudin (a Southeast Texas by way of New Orleans contribution) on page 207 and the Frito pie variation served by adventurous Austin pitmasters on page 201.

Speaking of brilliant and regional, the influence of our neighbor to the south cannot be overstated. Mexico and Texas are forever intertwined, and Texas is no doubt the benefactor, especially where food is concerned. It's impossible to imagine our culinary landscape without its Mexican accent, and it's particularly evident on our breakfast table, where our eggs and potatoes find their highest and best use beneath a spoonful of fiery salsa and our bread takes the shape of a hot-from-the-basket tortilla. The blessed trinity of eggs, tortillas, and chiles are the building blocks (among other delectable items) of everything from a simple breakfast taco to a mountainous plate of migas to a groaning platter of chilaquiles.

Nutritionists debate whether breakfast is indeed the most important meal of the day. I would humbly argue that in Texas, whether you're up before the sun rolling out biscuits or on your second Bloody Mary baking klobasniky, it's too good to skip.

Biscuits and Sausage Gravy

Nowadays biscuits seem to show up only on the menus of diners and haute-Southern restaurants. Biscuits eaten at home, alas, are all too often of the twist-open-tube variety. People are intimidated by scratch-made biscuits, afraid they court certain disaster with a fourth of a teaspoon too much here, two too many seconds of kneading there. Stephen Harrigan, writing about his love of the balls o' dough for *Texas Monthly* back in 1984, suggests reminding yourself that you're "merely the instrument through which the biscuits will find expression." And if you mess them up—if they don't rise to the occasion, so to speak—so what? Cream gravy hides a lot of flaws.

Makes 12 biscuits

For the biscuits

2 cups all-purpose flour

1 tablespoon baking powder

¼ teaspoon baking soda

½ teaspoon salt

2 tablespoons vegetable shortening, chilled

2 tablespoons unsalted butter, chilled

1 cup buttermilk, chilled

For the sausage gravy

½ pound breakfast sausage

½ cup all-purpose flour

4 cups whole milk, warm

Salt and ground black pepper

TO MAKE THE BISCUITS:

Preheat the oven to 450°F.

In a large bowl, combine the flour, baking powder, baking soda, and salt, then use your fingertips to quickly work the shortening and butter into the flour mixture; it should feel like coarse meal. Make a well in the flour mixture and add the buttermilk a little at a time, using a wooden spoon to stir just until a sticky dough forms.

Turn the dough onto a floured surface, sprinkle with flour, and knead gently, four or five times (you can add more flour if the dough is sticky). Press the dough out into a round about ½ inch thick, then use a floured biscuit cutter to cut out 12 biscuits.

Place the biscuits on a sheet pan so they just touch. Bake for about 15 minutes, turning the pan halfway through for even cooking, until the biscuits are raised and golden brown.

TO MAKE THE GRAVY:

Cook the sausage in a medium cast-iron skillet over medium heat until cooked through, then remove with a slotted spoon. Drain off all but 2 to 3 tablespoons of the fat (add vegetable oil to make up the difference if you don't have enough).

Add the flour and stir, scraping up any bits in the pan.

Slowly add the warm milk, whisking constantly until smooth. Lower the heat and continue to stir until the gravy is thick (if it's too thick, you can add a little warm water). Stir in the cooked sausage and season with salt and pepper.

Plate a couple of biscuits, cover them with a generous ladleful of gravy, and dig in.

Kolaches

We could have written a whole chapter on kolaches (and their meaty cousins, klobasniky). Interest in our beloved confection has been rising like a ball of warm dough. A treatise on the pillowy pastry made the pages of the *New York Times* in 2013, and nowadays it's possible to procure a kolache in Portland and Brooklyn and quite a few places in between. Here in Texas, we have our own Kolache Triangle, where motorists not so mysteriously disappear from the highways that connect San Antonio, Dallas, and Houston and reappear at one of the many longtime vendors that dot the area. A fresh-baked kolache, exuding butter and sugar and warm fruit, is no mere off-ramp diversion: it's a golden ticket back in time to Grandma's—or Babička's—kitchen.

Makes 2 dozen kolaches (1 sheet pan)

1 (¼-ounce) package
(2¼ teaspoons) active dry yeast

1 teaspoon sugar

1 cup warm water

1 cup (2 sticks) unsalted butter, softened, plus more for greasing the bowl

½ cup sugar

2 egg yolks

6 to 7 cups all-purpose flour, plus more for dusting

Melted butter, for brushing (you cannot use too much)

Kolache filling of choice (pages 200 to 207)

Special equipment: stand mixer

Combine the yeast, sugar, and warm water in a small bowl and whisk together. Let sit for 15 minutes; small bubbles should rise to the top. Grease a large bowl with butter.

In the bowl of a stand mixer, combine the butter, sugar, and egg yolks. Using the paddle attachment, beat on medium speed until the mixture becomes lighter in color, about 4 minutes.

Add the yeast mixture and 1 cup of flour to the stand mixer. Mix briefly to combine. Add 1 cup of flour at a time, mixing to combine between each addition. When the dough gets too stiff to work with the paddle attachment, swap it out for the dough hook. Keep adding flour until the dough is soft and almost sticky, but not so soft it falls off the dough hook. When you reach this point, knead the dough with the dough hook on medium speed for about 5 minutes. Transfer to the greased bowl, cover with a towel or plastic wrap, and let rise for 1 hour.

Brush a sheet pan with melted butter. Punch the dough down and divide into 24 equal-sized pieces. Shape each kolache into a ball and space evenly on the prepared pan. Brush with more melted butter. Cover with a towel and let rise for 1 hour.

Carefully form a divot in the center of each kolache. Don't push through the bottom of the dough, and make the divot large enough to hold a heaping tablespoon of filling. Add your favorite filling (see pages 200 to 207). Let sit for 10 minutes, while the oven heats up.

Preheat the oven to 400°F.

Bake the kolaches for 12 to 15 minutes, until golden. Remove from the oven and brush with more melted butter. Serve warm or at room temperature.

Kolache Fillings

Fruit Filling

One of the best things about fruit-filled kolaches is that they can be seasonal: make peach kolaches in early summer, fig in late summer, pumpkin in the fall, and strawberry in the spring. They're also a canvas for all kinds of combinations. Ginger-mango kolaches, anyone? Austin-based Dawn Orsak, a Texas-Czech food expert and veteran judge of kolache competitions, says the basic formula is the same: fruit, butter, and sugar, cooked until soft. If you use bigger fruit like apricot, fig, or prune, you'll need to break it up as it cooks with the back of a fork or a pastry cutter. "You want the consistency pasty," she says, "but not like a baby food puree."

Makes enough filling for 2 dozen kolaches (see page 198)

1 cup dried fruit, such as prunes, cherries, or peaches

1 cup boiling water

1 cup frozen fruit, of the same kind as the dried fruit

½ cup sugar

2 tablespoons unsalted butter

In a medium bowl, cover the dried fruit with the boiling water and let sit, covered, until cool.

In a small saucepan, combine the frozen fruit, dried fruit and its liquid, and sugar. Cook over medium heat, simmering, for 8 to 10 minutes, until slightly thickened.

Add the butter, stir it in to melt, and let the fruit mixture cool completely before using. Use the back of a spoon or a fork to break up the bigger chunks of fruit, if any.

Poppy Seed Filling

Kolache fillings are all over the map these days (which isn't a bad thing), but hard-core purists might say "Czech, please" if you offer them a kolache filled with anything other than apricots, prunes, cottage cheese, or poppy seeds.

Makes enough filling for 2 dozen kolaches (see page 198)

1½ cups milk

1 cup poppy seeds, pulsed a couple times in a coffee grinder or small food processor

1 cup sugar

1 tablespoon all-purpose flour

1 tablespoon unsalted butter

1 teaspoon vanilla extract

½ teaspoon salt

Bring the milk to a simmer in a large pot over medium-low heat. Whisk in the rest of the ingredients and cook, whisking constantly to prevent lumps, until thickened, about 3 minutes. Remove from the heat and let cool completely before using.

Frito Pie Filling

Savory kolaches are usually formed into klobasniky, enclosing sausages or other meaty fillings (like boudin, page 207) in sweet, yeasty kolache dough. But these, from beloved Austin barbecue joint LeRoy and Lewis, are formed like their sweet kolache cousins, open-faced, with a chili-filled divot in the center. A blizzard of cheese, onions, and chips completes this ode to the Frito pie.

Makes enough filling for 2 dozen kolaches

2 ancho chiles, stems removed

2 guajillo chiles, stems removed

2 árbol chiles, stems removed

2 cups boiling water

½ pound ground beef

1 teaspoon ancho chile powder

1 teaspoon ground cumin

1 teaspoon granulated garlic

1 teaspoon paprika

1 tablespoon salt

Unbaked dough from Kolaches (page 198)

¼ cup shredded cheddar cheese

2 tablespoons finely diced white onion

1 cup Fritos corn chips

Cover the chiles with the boiling water in a medium heatproof bowl and let steep for 10 minutes. Pour the chiles and their liquid into a blender and puree until smooth.

While the chiles steep, brown the ground beef in a medium saucepan over medium-high heat, stirring to break it up. Add the chile puree, ancho chile powder, cumin, granulated garlic, paprika, and salt to the ground beef. Bring to a simmer and cook over medium-low heat for about 20 minutes. Allow to cool before using as filling for kolache dough.

Preheat the oven to 400°F.

Form the kolaches according to the directions on page 198.

Bake the kolaches for 12 to 15 minutes, until golden. Remove from the oven and let cool for 5 to 10 minutes. While still warm, top the kolaches with the cheese, onion, and Fritos, and serve.

If It's Not Sweet, It's Not a Kolache

Just a week after moving to Columbia, Missouri, for graduate school, I had already conducted crucial field research. I knew which grocery store carried Topo Chico, where to find suitable Mexican food, and which bars served Lone Star. But I'd yet to scout out a staple of my diet since childhood: the sausage kolache.

In East Texas, where I grew up, every Shipley, Sunflower, and Snowflake I walked into carried at least a few varieties of the savory pastry. So in Columbia, I drove to a strip-center doughnut shop, hoping their kolaches would be at least passable.

"I'd like a kolache," I told the woman at the counter as I scanned the glass case of baked goods.

"A croissant?" she asked. I was in trouble.

"A kolache."

"We don't have any croissants."

For the next nine months, my life was devoid of something that had once been ubiquitous. But one day I found on my doorstep *The Homesick Texan's Family Table*, written by Texpat Lisa Fain, a Texas cooking expert and longtime friend of *Texas Monthly*. I eagerly flipped through the pages of the new tome, crisp and white, until I found a photo of what I wanted to make: a sinful, juicy link of kielbasa, hugged into dough, with pickled jalapeño and gooey melted cheese tumbling out of the bread cocoon.

But wait. There, in the prominent recipe title, was a word I had never seen before. What the heck was a klobasnek? That was my first realization that the kolache I (and thousands of other Texans) had ingested and loved for years was a delicious linguistic lie.

Texas-Czech communities clustered in the Central Texas Czech belt are well known as places to find authentic kolaches, which their forebears brought to the state in the 1800s. Filled with fruit and sometimes cheese—original flavors included apricot, prune, farmer's cheese, and poppy seed—these kolaches were and remain an integral part of Czech life. "Kolaches are part of our identity," says Dawn Orsak, a Texas-Czech lay folklorist. "In the same way that Italians would be proud of the way their mom made ravioli, or Mexican Americans, the way their mom made sopaipillas."

But it was the kolache's cousin, the klobasnek, which many believe was invented in Texas (more on this later), that worked its way into the morning routines of people across the state. By the nineties, the klobasnek (klobasniky in plural)—made from the same semisweet yeast dough as the traditional kolache but stuffed with kielbasa rather than fruit—had begun to proliferate across Texas, thanks to successful chains like the Kolache Factory, which began offering the "on the run" food to Houstonians in 1982. The popular franchise sold both kolaches and klobasniky but didn't bother to make the distinction between the two. It was all a kolache to the non-Czech Texan (and thus to me).

Fain believes that the klobasnek eclipsed the kolache

in popularity because of the Texan palate. "The sweet kolache is very similar to other pastries that are available, like Danish, whereas the pig-in-a-blanket thing is kind of unique," she says. "And, you know, we're Texans. We love our meat. And so something with sausage or bacon or brisket just maybe has more appeal."

The kolache/klobasnek misnomer irks many Czech-Texans. In December 2016 journalist Katey Psencik pleaded with ignorant consumers to put an end to it. "I call upon you, people of Central Texas, to stop referring to these meat-filled delicacies as kolaches, and call them by their rightful name: Klobasniky, or klobasnek in the singular," she wrote for the *Austin American-Statesman*. "The Czech community will thank you."

Orsak agrees. "If they can use the Czech word 'kolache,' they could use the Czech word 'klobasnek,'" she says. "I don't really get that, why they can't just call it the right thing. It bothers me, but it's probably too late at this point."

How, I thought, can we be so militant about what constitutes proper barbecue but manage to be so clueless when it comes to kolaches? With each of the savory pastries I consumed, was I aiding in the death of a key component of a vibrant Texas culture?

To finally get some answers, in 2014 I went to West, the kolache mecca just north of Waco, right off Interstate 35, to have svačina (Czech for "afternoon snack") with Mimi Montgomery Irwin. Until she died, in 2019, Mimi presided over the now closed Village Bakery, which her parents, Wendel and Georgia Montgomery, founded in 1952. Wendel is widely credited with the invention of the klobasnek, which Mimi said was a mash-up of the most American of foods, the hot dog, with a poppy seed kolache, the only variety at the bakery that was rectangular and enclosed, rather than circular with a divot for exposed filling at the top.

"My dad saw someone eating a hot dog, and it dawned on him," Mimi told me. "'We'll just take the kolache dough and put the little cut sausage in it and wrap it.' It was a little hot dog. And that's how it started." Wendel's creation was added to the rotation at the bakery in 1953.

Mimi didn't seem to share my obsession with how the name of the traditional Czech pastry was bastardized. But she shared her father's frustration that the two were conflated. "He never claimed it was the kolache," she said. "It infuriated him. That wasn't his mission. It was uniquely what it was, klobasniky—'little sausage.'"

But that unique creation has taken on many forms in the years since: some simple, such as swapping brisket for sausage, and others unconventional, like the egg-based versions that have become popular at some places. "My father would probably have been aghast at the idea," Mimi said. "I can understand it. It's the Egg McMuffin concept. It's the McDonaldization of a Czech food." Mimi, on the other hand, had pushed herself as far as she was willing to go. When she took over the bakery, she'd added klobasniky with cheese and jalapeños to the mix. But after that, she'd drawn a hard line. "It's not my mission in life to sell kiwi kolaches," she told me.

I left West full of dough and sausage and realization. Since discovering that I had been calling it by the wrong name, I had thought that my love of the klobasnek made me a clueless interloper into Czech culture. And I was, to be sure, but not because of my devotion to the klobasnek, which, after all, is a welcome addition to the Czech pastry canon. Calling a klobasnek a kolache isn't the chief battle in the Czech community, anyway. They're worried about a far greater loss: the disappearance of their traditions. "I'm working backwards from my worst-case scenario here, which is that in fifty years, no one who has a Czech background knows how to make them, and the only thing you can find is banana and Nutella kolaches or chicken enchilada," Orsak says.

The very least that I, an unabashed lover of both artisanal and doughnut shop klobasniky (apologies to the Czech community), can do is offer what people like Mimi and Orsak gave me: an education. The next time you have a hankering for a Philly cheesesteak "kolache," look for Czech-run bakeries in the area instead. And when you find them, force your untrained tongue to ask for a "klobasnek" rather than a "sausage kolache," which we both now know doesn't exist.—*Abby Johnston*

Boudin Klobasniky

These klobasniky come from 2022 James Beard Best Chef nominee Steve McHugh, the brains behind San Antonio's meat-centric and much-lauded Cured, as well as the new Landrace. McHugh spent the early part of his career in New Orleans, hence this Cajun spin on a Texas classic, in which the plump Louisiana sausage—usually savory ground pork, a profusion of white rice, and loads of seasoning—is gussied up with green chiles and rich chicken livers.

Makes enough filling for 1 sheet pan of klobasniky

1 pound pork shoulder, cut into large chunks

¼ pound chicken livers

1 tablespoon kosher salt

¼ cup diced white onion (about ¼ onion)

¼ cup diced poblano chile (about ½ chile)

¼ cup diced jalapeño chile (about 1 chile)

2 tablespoons diced celery (about ½ stalk)

1 tablespoon chopped garlic (about 4 cloves), plus 1½ teaspoons chopped garlic (about 2 cloves)

1 teaspoon ground black pepper

¼ teaspoon cayenne pepper

¼ teaspoon paprika

¼ teaspoon ground white pepper

½ teaspoon dried thyme

½ cup cooked white rice

¼ cup chopped green onions (about 3)

2 tablespoons chopped fresh flat-leaf parsley

1 recipe kolache dough (page 198)

Special equipment: a stand mixer

In a large bowl, combine the pork shoulder, chicken livers, salt, onion, poblano chile, jalapeño chile, celery, 1 tablespoon of the garlic, the black pepper, cayenne, paprika, white pepper, and thyme. Cover with plastic wrap and refrigerate for 24 hours.

The next day, place the pork mixture in a heavy-bottomed pot or Dutch oven and just barely cover with water. Bring the pot to a simmer, cover, and simmer for 2 hours.

Remove the mixture from the heat and let cool slightly. While still warm, pour the mixture into a mesh strainer set over a bowl, making sure to save the broth.

Place the pork mixture in a stand mixer and use the paddle attachment to break up the meat, about 30 seconds at medium-low speed.

Add the rice, green onions, and parsley and mix for 1 minute. Add half of the remaining broth (about 1 cup) and mix to fully incorporate, another 30 seconds. If the mixture seems dry, add more broth.

Let cool and taste for seasoning before stuffing into kolache dough. (Follow the instructions for baking kolaches on page 198.)

Note: For this preparation, you'll want to shape the dough differently than you would for the fruit-filled, open-faced kolaches on page 198. Roll each ball of dough into a 6 x 4-inch rectangle, and place a couple tablespoons of the filling in a line down the center of the dough. Fold the short ends up over the filling, and then the longer ends, pinching the dough together to seal. Place the klobasniky seam-side down and proceed with baking per the instructions.

Chilaquiles Poblanos

This breakfast dish of crispy tortillas swathed in a bright and creamy green sauce comes to us from Houston chef Victoria Elizondo, of Cochinita & Co. She recommends serving a big platter of these chilaquiles topped with fried eggs, sprinkled with cheese, and garnished with verdolagas (purslane) and pickled red onions. On the side, serve your favorite beans (may we recommend the Frijoles de Olla on page 84?).

Serves 4

For the pickled onions

½ red onion, diced

¼ cup distilled white vinegar

¼ cup water

Large pinch sugar

Large pinch salt

For the chilaquiles

3 large poblano chiles

1 quart cooking oil (avocado, canola, or corn)

15 corn tortillas, cut into 8 even triangles (4 if the tortillas are small)

Salt

1 cup heavy cream

1 cup chicken broth

½ large white onion, cut into thin strips

3 jalapeño chiles, stems removed, cut into thin strips

4 garlic cloves, minced

½ cup shredded queso chihuahua

4 eggs (or 1 to 2 eggs per person)

1 bunch fresh cilantro, chopped, for serving

1 bunch verdolagas (purslane), leaves picked from stem, for serving

Pickled red onions, for serving

TO MAKE THE PICKLED ONIONS:

Combine all the ingredients in a small skillet over medium heat. Bring to a boil and then cook for 3 to 4 minutes, or until the liquid has evaporated. Let cool.

TO MAKE THE CHILAQUILES:

Roast the poblano chiles over an open burner or under a broiler until their skin turns black (flip with tongs to get all sides). Immediately place in a sealed bag or container to lock in the steam. Let sit for 15 minutes, or until cool enough to handle.

Meanwhile, line a sheet pan or tray with paper towels. Heat all but 2 tablespoons of the oil in a small, deep pot over high heat and carefully drop in the tortilla triangles. Fry until golden, 2 to 3 minutes, turning them a few times for an even fry. Remove the tortilla chips and place on paper towels. Sprinkle with salt.

Remove the charred skin from the poblano chiles by rinsing off or wiping with a paper towel. Discard the stems and seeds. Dice the roasted chiles.

In a blender, puree half the poblano chiles with the heavy cream and chicken broth.

In a large skillet, heat the remaining 2 tablespoons oil over medium-high heat. Add the onion, jalapeño chiles, and garlic and cook until lightly browned, then add the poblano chile sauce.

Let the sauce simmer over low heat for 10 minutes, then add the rest of the roasted poblano chiles and the chips and stir until the chips are fully coated. Sprinkle with the cheese and cook until the cheese melts. Transfer to a serving dish.

Fry the eggs to your liking in a separate pan, then place on top of the chilaquiles. Sprinkle with cilantro, verdolagas, and pickled red onions.

Meat, Egg, and Cheese Breakfast Tacos

You can put just about anything in a breakfast taco—barbacoa or brisket, refried beans or rajas—but sometimes you're hungry for the sturdy, inexpensive, uncomplicated goodness that is the meat, egg, and cheese taco. A fixture of every taqueria menu, this beauty is almost always a warm flour tortilla stuffed with fluffy scrambled eggs, melty cheese, and your choice of bacon or sausage. It's a wholly (holy?) satisfying trinity of fillings that requires nothing more than a few spoonfuls of your favorite salsa.

Makes 1 breakfast taco (see Note)

2 tablespoons uncooked chorizo, breakfast sausage, or bacon (diced)

2 eggs

Pinch salt

Pinch ground black pepper

2 tablespoons shredded Oaxaca or Monterey Jack cheese

1 corn or flour tortilla

Salsa of your choosing, for serving

In a large skillet over medium-high heat, cook the meat, using a wooden spoon or spatula to break it into small pieces. Cook until browned, 3 to 4 minutes. Use a slotted spoon to remove the meat to a paper towel–lined plate, leaving any grease in the pan. Lower the heat to medium.

Crack the eggs into a bowl and whisk with the salt and black pepper. Add to the fat in the skillet and cook, stirring, until almost (but not quite!) set, about 2 minutes. While the eggs are still slightly wet, add the meat back into the pan and stir to combine. Turn off the heat.

Use the spatula to form the eggs into an oblong, taco-friendly shape. Cover with the cheese and let sit while you heat the tortilla in a separate skillet until just warm, about 1 minute. (You can also heat the tortilla in the microwave, but it won't be quite as tasty.)

Slide the eggs onto the tortilla, cheese-side up. Serve with salsa of your choice.

Note: You can multiply this recipe by as many breakfast tacos as you need to make; a standard 10-inch skillet will fit enough meat and eggs for 4 tacos.

ODE TO THE
Breakfast Taco

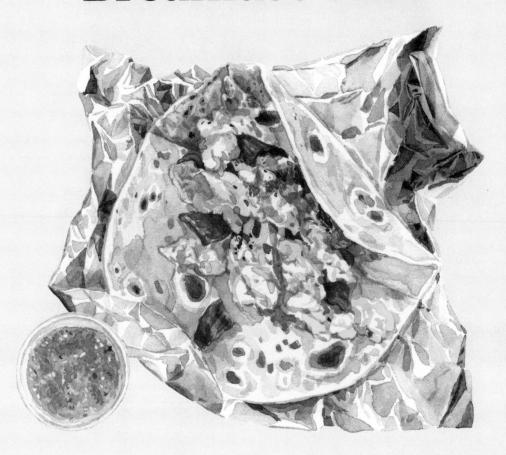

It's more exotic than a sandwich. It's healthier than a cheeseburger. It's portable, expertly wrapped in foil and stuffed into a paper to-go bag. It is one of the best bargains on earth, at $3 or less. And it's ubiquitous, so much so that it's hard to remember that it burst onto the Texas scene only some thirty years ago, when the Mexican workingman's breakfast migrated north and some anonymous saint had the smarts to marry the key elements of an American morning—scrambled eggs, bacon, potatoes—with the Mexican staples of salsa, cheese, refried beans, and tortillas. Behold the mighty breakfast taco. It is genius.

Yes, the name is a point of contention: usually, anything in a flour tortilla is a burrito, but because the word *burrito* arrived in some cities only as recently as the eighties, when the flour tortilla emerged as an alternative to corn, "taco" has remained the default term. (A general rule of thumb: If you're west of Brady, call it a "breakfast burrito"; if you're east, it's a "breakfast taco." In Laredo, it's a "mariachi," though nobody can conclusively say why.) Yet whether it comes from the taqueria in San Antonio that offers homemade chorizo, the hole-in-the-wall in El Paso that serves machaca, or the greasy spoon in Austin that throws in some potato hash, the breakfast taco is delicious—and the fuel that energizes the workforce, be it blue-collar, white-collar, or no-collar. I think we can agree on that.—*Katy Vine*

Mexican Scrambled Eggs

Said to signify the colors of the Mexican flag, the bright white onion, spicy green chile, and warm red tomato so enliven a skillet of scrambled eggs, we don't know why folks eat them any other way. Serve with warm tortillas and fresh salsa.

Serves 4

2 tablespoons canola oil

½ medium white onion, chopped

1 to 2 jalapeño or serrano chiles, stems removed, diced

2 plum tomatoes, chopped

8 eggs

Salt

Ground black pepper

Salsa, for serving

Warm tortillas, for serving

Heat the oil in a large skillet over medium heat. Add the onion and cook until softened and translucent. Reduce the heat to medium-low and add the chiles. Cook for about 1 minute, then add the tomatoes and cook for another minute.

In a large bowl, gently beat the eggs with a big pinch of salt. Add the eggs to the pan and cook until set. Season with salt and black pepper. Serve with salsa and warm tortillas.

Migas

This humble breakfast dish springs from the grand tradition of scraping together something out of nothing. It is one of many adaptations of a Spanish "peasant dish" that, in its simplest form, consists of bits of day-old bread panfried with garlic. In central Mexico, migas is a garlicky soup thickened with stale bolillos and amped up with pig parts. As for the version we Texans know and love, it's believed to hail from the border region, as so many good things do, and though it may be slightly less complex, it's no less soul-affirming.

Serves 4

8 eggs

½ teaspoon salt

½ teaspoon ground black pepper

3 tablespoons vegetable oil

4 corn tortillas, cut into strips

¼ cup diced yellow onion (about ¼ onion)

1 jalapeño chile, stem and seeds removed, minced

2 garlic cloves, minced

1 tomato, diced

½ cup shredded Monterey Jack cheese

Tortillas, for serving

1 avocado, sliced, for serving

Salsa, for serving

Whisk the eggs with the salt and pepper in a large bowl and set aside.

In a large cast-iron skillet or nonstick pan, heat the oil over medium-high heat. When it begins to shimmer, add the tortilla strips. Cook, stirring constantly, until crisped, about 1 minute. Use a slotted spoon to remove to a plate lined with paper towels. (There should be oil left over, but if not, you'll need to add some until you have about a tablespoon.)

Add the onion, chile, and garlic to the oil in the skillet and cook until softened, about 3 minutes. Add the eggs and cook, stirring. Just before the eggs set—you want them to still be slightly wet—add the tortilla strips and diced tomato. Stir to combine, remove from the heat, and sprinkle with the cheese. Serve with tortillas, avocado, and your favorite salsa.

CHAPTER 7

There Stands the Glass

BY JESSICA DUPUY

Because Texans Can't Live on Brisket, Tacos, and Rib Eyes Alone

Maybe it's our wiring, but Texans don't exactly need our arms twisted when it comes to having a big time with friends and family. And that big time invariably involves booze, whether it's Mexican martinis with colleagues at happy hour, ice-cold beers at an early afternoon tailgate, or mimosas at weekend brunch. Hell, we'll shake up a margarita anytime.

And if it's not in our wiring, it's certainly in our history. Vineyard plantings in Texas date as far back as the mid-1600s, when Spanish missionaries began to move northward from Mexico. Wine production in West Texas and New Mexico was fairly prolific by the time settlers headed west in search of gold on the Santa Fe Trail in the mid-nineteenth century (at the time, beer and wine were the better choices for hydration, considering the quality of the water). The longest continuously operating winery in the state, Val Verde, in Del Rio, began production in 1883, maintaining the right to make wine throughout Prohibition for sacramental purposes.

Texas was an early adopter of the temperance movement, passing statewide Prohibition in 1919, a full year before the Eighteenth Amendment went into effect. But Texans were not deterred. There are countless tales of determined imbibers making their way south of the border for bootleg sotol and tequila. Speaking of the latter, there are many claimants to the title of creator of the margarita (likely a version of the daisy cocktails popular in the early twentieth century, which consisted of a base spirit mixed with citrus and sugar). These include Santos Cruz, a bartender at the famed Balinese Room, in

Galveston, who named it for frequent performer Peggy Lee ("Peggy" being the diminutive of the name "Margaret"), and Margarita Sames, a Dallas socialite who said she invented it for a party at her second home, in Mexico.

One of the carryovers from the temperance movement was the silly notion of dry counties, wherein local leaders could impose their own restrictions on alcohol consumption. Once again, Texans worked around that by simply driving long distances to places that did sell booze. As of 2021, all but five counties and municipalities had abandoned their dry status, proving that as much as Texans love their brisket, enchiladas, and rib eyes, they also must insist on the appropriate pairings of wine, cocktails, and beer.

It's a golden age for drinking in Texas. If you're interested in Texas wine, there are more than four hundred permitted wineries to choose from in every corner of the state. Legions of craft beer makers have joined iconic breweries like Spoetzl, which produces the yellow-labeled Shiner Bock. Local distilleries are churning out everything from vodka, gin, rum, and whiskey to the aforementioned sotol that once had Texans running for the border. Bartenders across the state have embraced the pre-Prohibition craft cocktail craze, honoring the classics while weaving in innovative creations of their own. Of course, all of them can shake up the Texas originals, from the lemony vodka-based Chilton to the simple tequila-centric Ranch Water and Mexican martini. And you'll find recipes for those and more in this chapter. Cheers!

Classic Margarita

Innumerable are the creation stories associated with the margarita, and so too the opinions on how to drink one. Rocks or frozen? (Answer: up.) Mexican lime or Persian? Plata, reposado, or añejo? Salt or no? (*¡Claro que sí! ¡Un tequila sin sal es como un amor sin besos!*) As with many things, the best margarita is the one you like. That said, there's a pretty strong consensus as to the building blocks of a perfect margarita: tequila (preferably silver), lime juice (preferably from Mexican, or Key, limes), and orange liqueur (preferably Cointreau). The recipe below is a guideline, so experiment a little to find the ratio that suits your taste. The trick is getting all the components working in harmony. And since those components can vary widely (the limes alone are a crapshoot), it's a good idea to test your creation and make adjustments if needed. Finally, approach gingerly. This makes a wee, potent drink (like a martini, it's meant to be sipped from a small chilled glass). If you find it too strong, you can always go lighter on the tequila or serve it over ice.

Makes 1 cocktail

2 ounces 100-percent-agave silver tequila

Juice of 2 Mexican limes (about 2 ounces)

1 ounce orange liqueur, such as Cointreau

Salt, for the glass

Combine all the ingredients in a shaker, shake with cracked ice, and strain into a chilled, salt-rimmed coupe or martini glass.

Fruity Margaritas for a Crowd

In restaurants and bars, frozen margaritas come in every flavor of the neon-colored rainbow. But when we make them at home, we prefer to use actual fruit over the sweet syrups preferred by the sticky-floored dive bars that serve college students across the state. Strawberries are a classic, but peach, blackberry, and mango all work beautifully as well.

Makes 6 margaritas

1 cup blanco tequila

1 cup fresh lime juice

½ cup orange liqueur, such as Cointreau

¼ cup simple syrup (see Note)

2 cups frozen fruit of your choice

2 cups ice cubes

Lime wedges, for serving

Add all the ingredients except the lime wedges to a blender and blend until smooth.

Pour into glasses and garnish each with a wedge of lime.

Note: To make simple syrup, combine equal amounts of sugar and water in a saucepan and heat until the sugar is completely dissolved. Let cool and use, or store in the refrigerator until cocktail hour.

Fifty Years Ago a Texan Changed Happy Hour Forever

In the cantina the cocktail servers were adjusting their sequined miniskirts, while waitresses in black lace-up vests, gaucho pants, and tall boots chatted and laughed in the simulated moonlight of the dining room. A gregarious young man named Mariano Martinez rushed around in white leather bell-bottoms, setting out bottles of tequila and fresh limes. The date was May 7, 1971, and it was opening night of the much-anticipated Mariano's Mexican Cuisine, in the tony Old Town shopping center of Dallas. At five o'clock, the doors swung open, and the crowd surged in and immediately started ordering frozen margaritas. In less than two hours, everything had gone straight to hell.

It wasn't that everyone was drunk, but it did have to do with the margaritas. The first round was great, but pretty soon the bartenders were so backlogged they just started throwing ingredients in the blenders. No two drinks were alike, and everybody was complaining. One worker snapped at Martinez, "I've got cramps in my hands from squeezing those damn limes. I'm going back to Steak and Ale, where all they want is bourbon and Coke."

Martinez, now seventy-six, takes up the story he has recounted with gusto for five decades. "I tossed and turned all that night," he says. "The next morning I went to 7-Eleven for coffee and a pack of gum." While there, he glanced at the store's Slurpee machine, and "it came to me in a flash, like a gift from God." If that thing could make a slushy soft drink, surely it could make a frozen margarita. When the Southland Corporation, the parent company of 7-Eleven at the time, declined to sell him one, he and a mechanically minded friend named Frank Adams bought a used SaniServ soft-serve ice cream machine and lugged it to the restaurant. "We tinkered around with it," he remembers; they installed a stronger motor and compressor to swirl and chill the ingredients, and then Martinez experimented with different amounts of tequila, orange liqueur, and fresh lime juice. A few days later, on May 11, he covered the shiny stainless-steel box with wood-grain contact paper and set it on the bar. The icy green slush that would soon emerge was about to make cocktail history.

Born in Dallas in 1944, Martinez grew up in a family with deep roots in the Mexican restaurant business. His mother, Vera, was related to the Cuellar family, which founded the Dallas-based El Chico chain, in 1940. She worked as an administrative manager in the office of the

Oak Lawn location, and his father, Mariano, managed the upscale Lakewood-area restaurant.

In midcentury Texas, business and social success often depended on assimilation into the Anglo community. "The year before I started school," Martinez says, "we spoke only English at home, and my mother took my sister and me to Sanger's, sometimes even Neiman's, to buy clothes." They had a good life—a happy life—in spite of overt racism in Dallas, especially at school. In the sixth grade, Martinez recalls, "this white kid knocked me down, we started fighting, and he called me an 'effing Mexican.'" He hated school, with the exception of a single lesson, on inventors: "I remember vividly the day we learned about Thomas Edison and the Wright brothers. Afterward I thought, 'Oh, man, that's what I want to be.'"

Martinez dropped out of high school in tenth grade, and for a few years he lived in the fast lane, playing and singing in a band (thus the white leather bell-bottoms) and hoping for a music career. He had fun and made plenty of money, but he hedged his bets by getting a GED and a liberal arts degree from El Centro (now Dallas) College. When reality finally caught up with him, he took out a Small Business Administration loan, asked his grandmother for recipes, and turned to something he knew really well: the Mexican food business.

As it happened, 1971 was an excellent time to open a restaurant. More and more women were taking jobs outside the home, and families were dining out more often. Mexican immigrants, who provided the workforce for many of these new restaurants, were bringing recipes for then-exotic stuff like ceviche and mole poblano, adding to the state's beloved Tex-Mex repertoire of crispy tacos and cheese enchiladas. A fajita craze took hold and spread across the state, thanks in large part to "Mama" Ninfa Laurenzo's tacos al carbón. Most importantly, in April 1971, Texas legalized selling liquor by the drink in restaurants. No longer did diners have to tote bottles of booze to the table just to enjoy a cocktail.

Martinez was in the right place at the right time. A savvy media observer, he never passed up a chance to talk about his machine (at one point he had eleven of them at a single restaurant). When customers said, "You should have patented that thing—you'd be a billionaire!" he would smile and nod. "It would have been about as ridiculous as putting two carburetors in a '57 Chevy, painting on some flames, and trying to patent it," he says. Still, he was aware that he had kick-started a movement that was changing the restaurant industry. Not only had he helped take tequila from hooch to haute, he'd also invented something that would have a profound effect on the way people consume cocktails, from piña coladas to frozen daiquiris and everything in between.

Twenty years and an ocean of frozen margaritas later, Martinez retired the sturdy original contraption to a place of honor in one of his restaurants. Then, in 2003, he received an unusual solicitation. The Smithsonian Institution wanted to know if he'd consider donating that first machine to the National Museum of American History, in Washington, D.C. He agreed, of course, and a curator, Dallas-born Rayna Green, got busy. She researched the patent history of frozen drink makers, checked rival claims, and verified decades-old newspaper accounts. Her conclusion: His truly was the world's first frozen margarita machine. The honor "was beyond my dreams," Martinez says. When the day came to ship the machine, though, he was conspicuously absent. "I didn't go into work that day because I didn't want to see it leave the building," he says quietly.

Martinez's five restaurants keep him busy these days, though he lets his staff handle day-to-day operations. As for his modest little box, still covered in wood-grain contact paper, it sits on permanent display not far from Julia Child's kitchen. On the museum's website is a statement declaring that it stands at "the crossroads of a revolution" heralding the rise of regional Mexican food across America. To Martinez, though, it also represents a personal triumph. "It wasn't just a machine to me," he says. In some ways, "I'm still that little Mexican kid that got beat up in the sixth grade. It validated me, and that means a lot."—*Patricia Sharpe*

Mexican Martini

Warning: The Mexican martini you're likely to get in most bars nowadays is a mass-market impostor composed of premade margarita mix and delivered in a cloudy plastic shaker. Even worse, recipes for the home mixologist are all over the map, from nothing more than a top-shelf margarita with some olives to a syrupy abomination mixed with Sprite. Yuck. So, determined to right this wrong done to our state's most famous native cocktail, a group of otherwise sensible *Texas Monthly* employees experimented until they came up with something that jibes with what folks think they're drinking and what we think they ought to be. The result is a refreshing elixir in which smoky tequila squares off with salty olive brine while sweet orange liqueur plays mediator. Not particularly Mexican and not a martini, it is nevertheless a damn tasty, fittingly weird gift from Austin—supposedly its birthplace—to the rest of the world.

Makes 1 martini

3 ounces añejo tequila

1½ ounces orange liqueur, such as Cointreau

1½ ounces fresh lime juice

½ ounce green-olive brine from the jar

Splash of fresh orange juice

Salt, for the glass

Olives and lime wedges, to garnish

Combine the tequila, orange liqueur, lime juice, olive brine, and orange juice in an ice-filled shaker and shake vigorously.

Strain into a small, chilled coupe or martini glass rimmed with salt. Add a couple of olives and a lime wedge.

Proceed to drink slowly, preferably with a basket of chips and a bowl of salsa, and clear your calendar for the rest of the day.

Paloma

Come November, we Texans can't seem to get enough of our beloved grapefruit, the pride of the Rio Grande Valley, whose warm temperatures and loamy soils produce fruits that are vibrantly red, unusually sweet, and, as famed food writer R. W. Apple Jr. once described them, "fatter than a slow-pitch softball." And there's no better way to enjoy these golden globes than in conjunction with another of our favorite things: tequila. The result is a drink that is boldly smoky, tantalizingly tingly, and deliciously bittersweet.

Makes 1 cocktail

Salt, for the glass
2 ounces silver tequila
4 ounces fresh grapefruit juice
3 ounces Topo Chico
2 lime wedges

Salt the rim of a glass (some prefer to add a pinch of salt to the drink instead). Add the tequila, grapefruit juice, and Topo Chico. Squeeze and add the lime wedges, then fill the glass with ice and stir.

Note: You can add a little simple syrup (see page 222) or superfine sugar, if you prefer a sweeter Paloma.

ODE TO THE
Grapefruit

It's not entirely clear where grapefruit originated, but one thing is certain: Ruby Reds are native Texans. Back before the Roosevelt administration (the first one), all grapefruit was of a paler persuasion. But because these golden spheres of goodness don't cross-pollinate, mutant offspring eventually appeared, and one really hit the sweet spot. The red variety—born of a mutation found on a pink-grapefruit tree in McAllen in 1929—flourishes in the temperate Rio Grande Valley's sandy soils, its striking crimson flesh tinted from the antioxidant lycopene (also found in tomatoes) and its skin reminiscent of an Amarillo sunset. In 1934, the beloved orb was the first grapefruit to be granted a U.S. patent, under the name Ruby Red. And in the early nineties it was designated the official fruit of the Lone Star State. Coming into season in the fall, the dimpled fruits are a delicious way to survive the winter months, particularly when recruited to star in one of our favorite bittersweet cocktails, the Paloma.—*Shannon Stahl*

Ranch Water

With a mere three ingredients, this fizzy highball with fuzzy origins (both Austin and West Texas lay claim to it) couldn't be simpler. An explosion in popularity in recent years has inspired a glut of canned versions, but none compare to a homemade Ranch Water. Evoking a stripped-down, bubbly margarita, it's dry, bracing, and the perfect refresher for our hot summers.

Makes 1 cocktail

1 lime
2 ounces blanco tequila
½ cup Topo Chico

Cut a wedge out of the lime. Squeeze the rest of the lime juice into a tall glass filled with ice.

Add the tequila. Top with the Topo Chico and garnish with the lime wedge.

Note: If you like your Ranch Water a little sweeter, add an ounce or so of orange liqueur.

Chilton

The Chilton is a bracing, lemony cocktail allegedly born of a thirsty Lubbock doctor and a country club bartender who conspired to come up with a refreshing South Plains potable. Of course, pinning down origin stories is next to impossible, so the legend of Dr. Chilton and his zesty creation remains a rumor. But lending credence to the story is the fact that the drink—vodka, lots of lemon juice, bubbly water, and a salted rim—is virtually unheard of outside West Texas. That's too bad, because the Chilton is sunshine in a glass, a gloriously simple beverage that's as dry (no pun intended) and unpretentious as its presumed homeland.

Makes 1 cocktail

Salt, for the glass

1½ ounces vodka

Juice of 1 lemon (about 1½ ounces), plus an additional lemon wheel or wedge, for garnish

Soda water, to top

Rim a highball glass with salt, then fill with ice. Add the vodka and lemon juice. Fill the glass with soda water and stir gently. Garnish with a lemon wheel or wedge.

Michelada

Every good Texan knows that beer is a fine and proper antidote to the heat of summer, but why not spice things up—literally—with a michelada: a fizzy Mexican lager bedazzled with salt, lime, vinegary hot sauce, and some sort of umami-laden seasoning to be determined by whoever is mixing up the drink. There are those who like their "beertail" dead-simple, with just lime juice and salt. Others go nuts with secret ingredients and elaborate garnishes. This recipe sits squarely in the middle: not too complicated, not too basic, just right.

Makes 1 michelada

1 tablespoon chile lime salt, such as Tajín

1 tablespoon kosher salt

1 lime wedge, plus the juice of ½ lime

1 tablespoon tomato juice

2 teaspoons hot sauce (bartender's choice)

½ teaspoon Worcestershire sauce

Dash Maggi sauce

1 (12-ounce) can Mexican-style lager

On a plate, combine the chile lime salt and kosher salt and mix together. Wet the rim of a glass with the lime wedge and roll the edge of the glass in the salt mixture.

Fill the glass with ice. Add the lime juice, tomato juice, hot sauce, Worcestershire sauce, and Maggi sauce. Stir to combine. Top off with the beer and serve. If there's beer left in the can, serve it alongside the michelada.

Yaupon Avenue

This cocktail from Houston's Alba Huerta (pictured on page 219), owner of the cocktail bar Julep, is an ode to Texas-specific ingredients. The gin is infused with the leaves of the yaupon holly, a native plant. Sotol is an agave-derived spirit made from *dasylirion wheeleri*, also called desert spoon, a shrub that grows in the Chihuahua Desert of Mexico and West Texas. Grapefruit bitters are a nod to the legendary Rio Grande Valley fruit. You can buy all these ingredients at good-quality liquor stores across the state (if you can't find the dried lemon wheels, you can purchase from an online specialty store or find a recipe for making your own).

Makes 1 drink

1½ ounces Waterloo Old Yaupon Gin

½ ounce sotol

½ ounce agave nectar

½ ounce fresh lemon juice

½ ounce pineapple juice

2 dashes hopped grapefruit bitters

1 dehydrated lemon wheel, for garnish

Add all the ingredients except the lemon wheel to a shaker full of ice. Shake thoroughly and double strain, first through the shaker's strainer and then through a fine-mesh strainer held over a coupe glass. Garnish with the lemon wheel.

Acknowledgments

You can't put together any cookbook, and certainly not *The Big Texas Cookbook*, without a whole lot of help. To chronicle the foodways of a state as large as Texas is a formidable task (indeed it feels as if we barely scratched the surface). For an endeavor like this one, there is no such thing as too many cooks in the kitchen.

Speaking of cooks, this book would not have come together without Paula Forbes (shout-out to Kathy Blackwell, a *Texas Monthly* executive editor, for the brilliant idea of bringing her on board). Paula is a longtime *Texas Monthly* collaborator, author of *The Austin Cookbook: Recipes and Stories from Deep in the Heart of Texas*, and editor of the digital newsletter *Stained Page News*, an exhaustive collection of all things related to cookbooks and those who love them. Drawing on her deep well of expertise and considerable Texas connections, she helped us dream up the scope of this book over a long afternoon that included a few rounds of drinks at the Driskill Bar, in Austin, and about four hundred sticky notes. She then reached out to chefs, food writers, and home cooks; collected a medley of recipes and some stories to go along with them; developed many recipes herself to round out the collection; and spent months holed up in her home kitchen, sautéing, stewing, frying, smoking, grilling, and so on, making sure every recipe came together as it should.

Paula cast a wide net over a wide state, and we are so grateful to the chefs and home cooks who agreed to contribute their knowledge and recipes: Tatsu Aikawa, Nicola Blaque, Damien Brockway, Misty David, Todd David, Victoria Elizondo, Cassandra Fortson, Raymundo Garcia, Christine Ha, Meena Habbu, Ranganath "Ron" Habbu, Jalen Heard, Alba Huerta, Nupohn Inthanousay, PJ Inthanousay, David Kirkland, Evan LeRoy, Steve McHugh, Lane Milne, Don Nguyen, Theo Nguyen, Tony J. Nguyen, Hugo Ortega, Alex Padilla, Alejandro Paredes, Margarito Pérez, Lisa Perini, Tom Perini, Anastacia Quiñones-Pittman, Janie Ramirez, Jonny Rhodes, Edgar Rico, Beto Rodarte, Julian Rodarte, Ernest Servantes, Chris Shepherd, Donny Sirisavath, Bob Somsith, Reyna Vazquez, Maritza Vazquez, Miguel Vidal, Michelle Wallace, Jonny White, Laurie Williamson, and Joe Zavala. Thanks also to the many *Texas Monthly* staffers who contributed cherished family recipes in the early selection process.

Many thanks to Anna Walsh, *Texas Monthly*'s director of editorial operations and our MVP, who kept everyone calm, gently nudged when necessary, and stepped up to the plate whenever we needed her. Erin Kubatsky, senior operations manager, provided vital help in drafting deadlines and—with the legal counsel of the invaluable Patricia Totten—wrangling contracts and permissions.

Texas Monthly is a writer's magazine, first and foremost, and this book is a reflection of that. Thank you to David Courtney (aka the Texanist), Jessica Dupuy, Joe Galván, Dan Goodgame, Abby Johnston, Prudence Mackintosh, Emily McCullar, June Naylor, José R. Ralat, Patricia Sharpe, Dan Solomon, Shannon Stahl, Daniel Vaughn, Katy Vine, and Christian Wallace, whose words in *The Big Texas Cookbook* illuminate the culture, history, idiosyncrasies, and joys of Texas cuisine.

It's said we eat with our eyes first, and creative director Emily Kimbro and her art department, in particular design director Victoria Millner and art producer Darice Chavira, made this cookbook a visual feast. Emily and Victoria crafted a vision for this beautiful book, and Darice's diligent planning and organization ensured that it would come to fruition. Thank you to photographer and longtime *Texas Monthly* collaborator Jody Horton, whose lush photos capture the essence of Texas food culture like no other. Thanks also to Harper Wave's Joanne O'Neill, who designed the cover, and Bonni Leon-Berman, who designed the interior pages.

There's an abundance of cookbooks out in the world, and the fact that you're reading this one is likely due to the efforts of the talented marketing and publicity professionals who helped spread the word about it. Thank you especially to Jessica Gilo and Amanda Pritzker on the HarperCollins marketing team; Yelena Nesbit, in publicity for HarperCollins; *Texas Monthly*'s Madison Bunner, Jalaane Levi-Garza, Tori Mohn, and Scott Ray; and our publicity team at Jackson Spalding.

Harper Wave's editorial director, Julie Will, provided a calm presence and thoughtful edits, always looking out for the reader as this cookbook came together. Thank you to Leda Scheintaub for the careful copy edit, and to Emma Kupor for the cheerful editorial assistance. Thanks also to our agent, Amy Hughes, of Amy Hughes Agency, for connecting *Texas Monthly* with Harper Wave.

Finally, many thanks to *Texas Monthly*'s editor in chief, Dan Goodgame, who not only contributed perhaps the funniest quote to the book but also laid the groundwork for it, helping conceptualize the conceit and inspiring us to imagine just how big a Texas cookbook could be. He tirelessly leads the charge for telling Texas stories in more forms and ways than ever before, a goal made possible by the magazine's owner, Randa Duncan Williams; president, Scott Brown; and the incredible, dedicated work of everyone at *Texas Monthly*.

—*Courtney Bond, executive editor, Texas Monthly*

Index

Buttermilk-Fried Chicken Liver and Caramelized Onion Po'boys, 174–75, *176–77*

Julep, Houston, 236

About the Author

Since 1973, *Texas Monthly* has chronicled life in contemporary Texas, publishing long-form literary storytelling on the state's most interesting characters and trends, along with reporting and analysis on vital issues such as politics, the environment, business, and education. Recognized for its editorial excellence and outstanding design, *Texas Monthly* is one of the most respected publications in the nation and has won fourteen National Magazine Awards.

HarperCollins books may be purchased for educational, business, or sales promotional use. For information, please email the Special Markets Department at SPsales@harpercollins.com.

FIRST EDITION

All photographs are © by Jody Horton. Food styling by Olivia Caminiti. Illustrations by Melinda Josie.

Designed by Bonni Leon-Berman

Library of Congress Cataloging-in-Publication Data has been applied for.

ISBN 978-0-06-306856-8

22 23 24 25 26   TC   10 9 8 7 6 5 4 3 2 1

Since 1973, **TexasMonthly** has chronicled life in contemporary Texas, publishing long-form literary storytelling on the state's most interesting characters and trends, along with reporting and analysis on vital issues such as politics, the environment, business, and education. Recognized for its editorial excellence and outstanding design, *Texas Monthly* is one of the most respected publications in the nation and has won fourteen National Magazine Awards.